Organ at St. Johannis, Oederquart

ARP SCHNITGER, ORGAN BUILDER

CATALYST FOR THE CENTURIES

Peggy Kelley Reinburg

BLOOMINGTON

INDIANA UNIVERSITY PRESS

Manufactured in the United States of America

Library of Congress Cataloging in Publication Data

Reinburg, Peggy Kelley, 1936-
Arp Schnitger, organ builder.

Bibliography: p.
Includes indexes.
1. Schnitger, Arp, 1648-1719. 2. Organ-builders–Biography. I. Title.
ML424.S36R4 786.5'092'4 [B] 81-47829
ISBN 0-253-30927-1 AACR2
1 2 3 4 5 86 85 84 83 82

Lovingly dedicated
to my parents
Anne McKee and *Wesley Thomas Kelley*
who encouraged an inquisitive musician
and
to *Lynn Fulk*
with gratitude for the music
and friendship we share

. . . why abandon a belief
merely because it ceases to be true.
Cling to it long enough, and not a doubt
It will turn true again, for so it goes.
Most of the change we think we see in life
Is due to truths being in and out of favor.

—Robert Frost, "The Black Cottage"

Contents

Preface xiii
Acknowledgments xv

Introduction 1

1. PRE-SCHNITGER PATRIARCHS 5

Ostfriesland 5
Hamburg 10
Oldenburg 12

2. MEASURE OF THE MAN 25

1680–1689 26
1690–1699 31
1700–1719 40

3. DEBT TO THE PAST 71

Stade: St. Cosmae 72
Neuenfelde: St. Pankratius 78
Steinkirchen 81
Norden: St. Ludgeri 85

4. LEGACY FOR THE FUTURE 102

Dedesdorf: St. Laurentius 103
Strückhausen: St. Johannes 108
Ganderkesee: St. Cornelius und Cypranius 110
Rastede: St. Ulrich 115

Appendix A *Chronological Listing of Schnitger's Organ Projects* 123

Appendix B *Scalings for Representative Schnitger Organs*
Nieuw Scheemda: Hervormde Kerk, I/8 131
Dedesdorf: St. Laurentius, II/12 132
Steinkirchen, II/P 28 140

Bibliography 147
Notes 149
Glossary of German Technical Terms 155
Index of Organs for Which Specifications Are Given 163
General Index 165

Plates

Organ at St. Johannis, Oederquart	Frontispiece
1. Coats of arms of Schnitger and his wife	3
2. Organ at Patrozinium Kirche, Rysum	16
3. Prospekt from organ at Scheemda	17
4. Church of St. Werenfridus, Osteel	18
5–9. Organ at St. Werenfridus, Osteel	18–19
10. Organ at St. Jacobi, Hamburg	20
11. Organ at St. Georg, Sengwarden	21
12. Map of Oldenburg	22
13–16. Organ at St. Laurentius, Langwarden	23–24
17, 18. Organ at St. Petri und St. Pauli, Cappel	51
19, 20. Church of St. Stephan, Schortens	52
21–25. Organ at St. Stephan, Schortens	53–55
26. Drawing for organ at Wittmund	56
27. Organ at Hohenkirchen	57
28. Main organ at Marienkirche, Lübeck	58
29. Organ at St. Johannis, Magdeburg	59
30–32. Organ at Hervormde Kerk, Noordbroek	60–61
33–36. Organ at Hervormde Kerk, Nieuw Scheemda	62
37. Organ at St. Bartholomäus, Golzwarden	63
38–40. Organ at Hervormde Kerk, Pieterburen	64–65
41. Christian V of Denmark	66
42. Console of the Dom organ, Lübeck	66
43. Organ at St. Willehad, Accum	67
44–47. Organ at Hervormde Kerk, Uithuizen	68
48. Sophie Charlotte, queen of Prussia	69

49. Friedrich I, king of Prussia 69
50. Organ at Eosander-Kapelle, Berlin 70
51–54. Organ at St. Cosmae, Stade 95–97
55. Steeple of St. Cosmae, Stade 97
56. Vincent Lübeck 97
57, 58. Organ at St. Pankratius, Neuenfelde 98
59. Hof des Orgelbauers, Neuenfelde 99
60. Organ at St. Ludgeri, Norden 99
61–64. Organ at Steinkirchen 100–101
65. Dedesdorf contract 104–105
66–70. Organ at St. Laurentius, Dedesdorf 119–21
71. Organ at St. Cornelius und Cyprianus, Ganderkesee 122

Map showing locations of Schnitger's organ projects
6–7

Preface

THIS book is not intended to enter the "Which is best?" fray or to serve as a purist's podium, for any controversy regarding superiority is unnecessary when several approaches to organ design have contributed so much to mankind's aesthetic development. Also, since the foremost organ builders and their disciples designed organs for specific acoustical situations and as vehicles for different styles of organ composition, it is only logical that we should extract the best from each as tools for learning and thus broaden our own sensitivities.

Purity and clarity of individual ranks, the consistent silvery sheen of the aliquots (mutations), and the often chilling mixtures of Schnitger and his tradition reign supreme when one sits in a North German church with an ear only to tonal analysis. Whether it be the Schnitger Rohrflöte 8′ and Spitzflöte 2′ at Ganderkesee; the thrilling Posaune 16′ at Steinkirchen; Norden's marvelous Waldflöte 2′, Quinte 1½′, and 4-rank Scharf; the Sesquialtera at Dedesdorf; or the unique Krummhorn 8′ at Stade's St. Cosmae, the sounds seem pared to their essence and perfectly capable of transporting us, at least momentarily, out of our frequently mundane surroundings to a higher plane of existence.

To delve beneath the surface of the art of Arp Schnitger serves only to entangle one in a web of prospective investigation sufficient to occupy a lifetime. My investigation commenced during the summer of 1974 while I was attending the Internationale Orgeltagung in Oldenburg, North Germany.

The summers of 1976 and 1978 afforded me the opportunity to examine, play, photograph, and record this master's instruments under the enlightening guidance of Fritz Schild, president of the Alfred Führer Orgelbau of Wilhelmshaven, a firm that has been responsible for the restoration of numerous historical North German organs. Such an opportunity is more than humbling when one realizes that of the 169 organs in which Schnitger's actual involvement as a builder has been documented, only 41 were to some degree extant in 1970. Those whose appetites are whetted may secure information regarding first-hand observation of the extant Schnitger organs from Harald Vogel, Direktor, Norddeutsche Orgelakademie, Grosse Strasse 1, D-2802 Ottersberg 1, West Germany.

This book assumes a minimal knowledge on the part of the reader of the *Werkprinzip*, of stop designations, and of the functions of the major components of a mechanical action organ. Background material on these technical aspects can be found in such sources as the Introduction to Peter Williams, *The European Organ, 1450–1850*; Poul-Gerhard Andersen, *Organ Building and Design*; and Hans Klotz, *The Organ Handbook*.

Throughout this book the following pitch designations have been used:

Acknowledgments

THE seeds for this project were sown in my undergraduate days by my very scholarly organ professor, Jean Slater Edson; and the resultant love for research was put to the test by Richard Enright, as I pursued graduate studies at Northwestern University. Johannes H. Schroeder, whose encouragement through many years led me to the 1974 Internationale Orgeltagung of the Gesellschaft der Orgelfreunde in Oldenburg; Ricklef Orth, Kirchenmusiker of the Auferstehungskirche in Oldenburg, who took me under his wing; Fritz Schild, Orgelbaumeister, now president and tonal director of the Alfred Führer Orgelbau in Wilhelmshaven, who has opened for me the doors to so many Schnitger organs; and Charles N. Henderson, editor of *The American Organist*, who first afforded me the opportunity to publish on the subject of Schnitger, encouraged me to write this book, and then granted me permission on behalf of The American Guild of Organists to reprint those portions of this work that first appeared in 1977 in *Music* (now *The American Organist*): all are directly responsible for my completion of this project. I am also indebted to:

the late Gustav Fock, author of *Arp Schnitger und seine Schule*, who forged the path for others;

Hilde Michalik Vogel, my dear friend and neighbor, who spent many weeks translating material with me;

Gottfried Doerfel, secretary of the Alfred Führer Orgelbau;

Jean Slater Edson and Richard Root for their translations of German from centuries past;

Letha Dreyfus, who put aside her flute to type the articles for *Music*;

James Mebane Reinburg, for Xeroxing reams of notes and drafts;

Jane Bruce, my "Renaissance" friend who first shared Germany with me;

Rebecca Reames, my former student, who first shared the Schnitger organs with me;

F. Dallas Peel, who processed many of my photographs with tender care;

Deborah Peel, also my former student, who contributed photographs taken during the course of her apprenticeship with the Alfred Führer Orgelbau;

Adrianus de Groot, avid Dutch researcher, who shared with me his knowledge of his country's wealth of Schnitger history;

Rodney Schrank of Concordia Publishing House, friend and advisor;

the many gracious organists in North Germany and the Netherlands who have permitted me access to their charges;

my young son, Alexander, whose patience has helped his mother realize a dream;

and to Lynn Fulk, whose many months of typing and proofreading afforded me practice time for recital performances.

Particular appreciation is given the following for permission to quote or to translate material from the sources noted:

Bärenreiter Verlag, Kassel and Frau Franziska Fock, Hamburg: *Arp Schnitger und seine Schule*;

Gerhard Stalling Verlag, Oldenburg, Germany: *Die Orgeln alten Herzogtums Oldenburg*;

Verlag Ostfriesische Landschaft, Aurich, Germany: *Die Orgeln Ostfrieslands*;

Stichting Groningen Orgelland, The Netherlands: *Arp Schnitger en zijn werk in het Groningerland*;

Karl Dieter Wagner Verlag and Helmut Winter, Hamburg: *Die Huss-Orgel in Stade* and *Die Schnitger-Orgel in Cappel*;
Evangelische-Luth. Landeskirchenamt Hannover: specifications of the Steinkirchen organ;
and Niedersächsisches Staatsarchiv, Oldenburg: numerous documents and correspondence.

I have endeavored to acknowledge all material quoted from those writers on Arp Schnitger who have preceded me.

The author and publishers express gratitude to the following for supplying and/or granting permission for the reproduction of illustrations appearing herein:

Johannes Wiegers, Heeslingen-Steddorf, Germany: frontispiece;
Franziska Fock, Hamburg, Germany: plates 1, 29, 56;
Foto-Commissie, Rijksmuseum, Amsterdam, The Netherlands: plate 3;
Deborah Peel, Richmond, Virginia; plates 4, 5, 13, 30, 31, 46;
Hans-Bernd Rödiger, Friedeburg, Ostfriesland, Germany: plates 11, 27, 43;
Niedersächsische Staatsarchiv, Oldenburg, Germany: plates 12, 41, 65;
Frithjof Fanöe Industrielfotografie, Wilhelmshaven, Germany: plates 16, 21, 71;
Verlag Oliva, Cuxhaven, Germany: plates 18, 54, 55;
Fritz Schild, Wilhelmshaven, Germany: plates 22, 23, 24, 25;
Verlag Ostfriesische Landschaft, Aurich, Germany: plate 26;
Photo-Appel, Lübeck, Germany: plate 28;
Adrianus de Groot, Washington, D.C.: plates 32, 38, 39, 40;
Foto-Meyer, Wilhelmshaven, Germany: plate 37;
Walter Steinkopf, Deutscher Kunst Verlag, Berlin, Germany: plates 48, 49;
KIM, Berlin, Germany: plate 50;
Kurt Lueders, La Celle, St. Cloud, France: plates 51, 60, 61;
Rebecca Reames, Arlington, Virginia: plate 59;
and Verlag Keller & Burkardt, Munich, Germany: plate 66.

The remaining photographs were taken by the author. Cathryn L. Lombardi produced the map showing the locations of Schnitger's organ projects.

Arp Schnitger Orgelmacher mpria

Introduction

ARP Schnitger's successful development owed much to the climate of the era following the Thirty Years' War; however, his outstanding personality and skill were the prime factors in his success, and organization was his forte. Evidence of the quality of his general education (which was better than that of the majority of his contemporaries in the profession) is to be found in the accuracy of his opinions and the precise manner in which his contracts were worded. Schnitger always employed the *manu propria* ("mpp.") of the scholar rather than the customary *mein eigen Hand* ("my own hand") when signing his contracts, although we note that even with educated persons there abounded inconsistencies in the spelling of names. Until about 1695, when Schnitger was 47, his signature usually appeared as "Schnittker" or "Schnitker." Then, even on some receipts for final payments, he used "Schnitger," a spelling that differed from that which appeared on earlier, related papers.[1]

In his contracts, as well as in his correspondence, the two foremost characteristics of the man Schnitger are evident—his devout nature and his basic unselfishness. The inscription "Soli Deo Gloria" is to be found on many of his organs; and he was accustomed to writing across the pages of his manuscripts such invocations as "In the name of Jesus, amen"; "My God, let me merit an honest life and blessed death, amen"; "Dear God and Father, enrich my soul so I may have all I need here and in eternity, amen." This faith carried him even in the face of the death of his eldest son, Arp, for in that same year he headed notes on the construction of the new organ for St. Michaelis Kirche in Hamburg with the words: "Everything depends on God's blessing. May the great God in whose name this is begun bless the means and help toward a happy conclusion."[2]

Schnitger was the benefactor of numerous poorer parishes and frequently supplied organs below cost, again for the "Glory of God." In 1699 he gave to his Lutheran friends in Groningen a small, one-manual organ. When the church council presented him with an honorarium of 100 Rtl., he added a second manual and three bellows. Always concerned with the maintenance of his instruments, he would occasionally revisit his earlier works and suggest means of correcting small deficiencies so that future generations might be assured of enjoying those organs. Jealously guarding his reputation, Schnitger was moved to extreme anger by unfair criticism. Klingenberg, the organist of the Jakobikirche in Stettin, derelict in his own weekly duty of tuning the Schnarrwerke (reed stops), complained of a defect in the Schnitger organ. Outraged, the builder retorted to the Stettin churchwardens: "If a major defect would appear, I would come, even if I had to walk—Herr organist Klingenberg blames the organ builder for something he himself failed to do. God usually punishes such fellows as employ similar tricks. I promise to answer for your Jakobi organ as long as I live."[3]

In 1693, during a somewhat prosperous period in his career, Schnitger had relinquished 800 Mk. interest due him from his home church in Neuenfelde for some property surrounding the church. It was because of this generosity that the churchwardens ceded to him and his heirs the vacant place to the south rear of the altar, hoping that the master would add another gem to the interior decoration of the new church. So he did, by commissioning his friend, the renowned Hamburg woodcarver Christian Precht, to create not only the Schnitger pew but also one for the Provost von Finckh. Both were decorated with coats of arms, Schnitger's displaying the compass (professional symbol of the organ builder), an arm emerging from the clouds to signify that the art of organ building was bestowed on him from heaven, and a helmet emblazoned with two crossed tuning horns, like the ones used for tuning organ pipes. His wife's crest includes a flower with three blossoms and three ears of wheat, symbolizing her inherited farm.

1. Artist's rendition of the coats of arms of Arp Schnitger and of his first wife.

Schnitger displayed the utmost conscientiousness in business dealings and strove to maintain his clients' respect. On February 1, 1694, in the midst of political unrest in Hamburg, he wrote the following letter to the Dombaumeister (master builder of the cathedral) in Bremen:[4]

> NOBLE, MOST HONORED HERR BAUMEISTER:
> It is with great concern that I have learned my letter has not reached you, in which I informed you regarding the cost of the wood for the organ base in your cathedral. No sooner had I arrived here from Bremen than I encountered unrest

> among the inhabitants, so that nothing could be accomplished. When the unrest had subsided, I immediately did my utmost to negotiate with the lumber dealers here in Hamburg, as well as with those in Altona and those living beyond the dike gate. These prices I communicated at once to my Herr Baumeister after the riots were over. You will please not hold it against me that the letter did not reach you. This I wanted to report quickly, sincerely offering my services at your command. With that, my humble greetings, commending you to God's care, I remain, my Herr Baumeister's most obedient servant.
>
> ARP SCHNITKER

In a request to the Swedish government in Stade for building privileges, Schnitger emphasized that he "would like, without vanity, to be regarded in such a way that nothing remained to be desired of his person, work and circumstances."[5] That Schnitger and his work *were* respected in his lifetime is evident from the geographical expanse of his opuses. Church and municipal records chronicle organs from Flensburg in the far north to Stettin and Moscow in the east, Portugal in the south, and England to the west, a truly amazing impact for a workshop of the Baroque era.

One must examine his heritage, his training, his ambitions, his successes and disappointments, the fruits of his labors, the joys and sorrows of his personal life, and the achievements of his pupils and successors. Perhaps then, a flesh-and-blood Arp Schnitger will emerge. Perhaps then, we shall appreciate even more the genius of the man who, above all others, influenced the greatest period of flowering in the history of the art of organ building.

The sight of such a monument is like a continuous and stationary music.
—Mme. de Staël

1. Pre-Schnitger Patriarchs

THE political battles between the Netherlands and Spain, the attitude of the Reformation toward the organ, and the relocations necessitated by the Thirty Years' War resulted in wider exposure and impact than would have normally been expected of Arp Schnitger's major predecessors in Hamburg, Ostfriesland, and Oldenburg. Travesties against the organ ranged from Zwingli's personal supervision of the destruction of the Zurich Grossmünster instrument in 1527, to pronouncements from the Synods of Holland and Zeeland in 1574 and from Middleburg in 1581 banishing organs and *all* instrumental music, to Luther's occasional moderate attacks relating the organ to Roman "trappings." Despite the forced mobility of many Dutch and German organ builders and the resultant overlapping of territories "occupied" by various builders, three rather distinct groups of sixteenth- and seventeenth-century organ craftsmen emerge from the scarce and often sketchy records. The records that remain for the period up to 1660 are extremely fragmentary; i.e., organists' names are listed with no affiliation, and organs are listed without builders. From 1660 on, the sources became much more detailed and almost all the churches, particularly those in the Oldenburg duchies, maintained archives.

Ostfriesland

From about 1550 through 1625 the Netherlands organ builders dominated the scene in Northwest Germany, just as

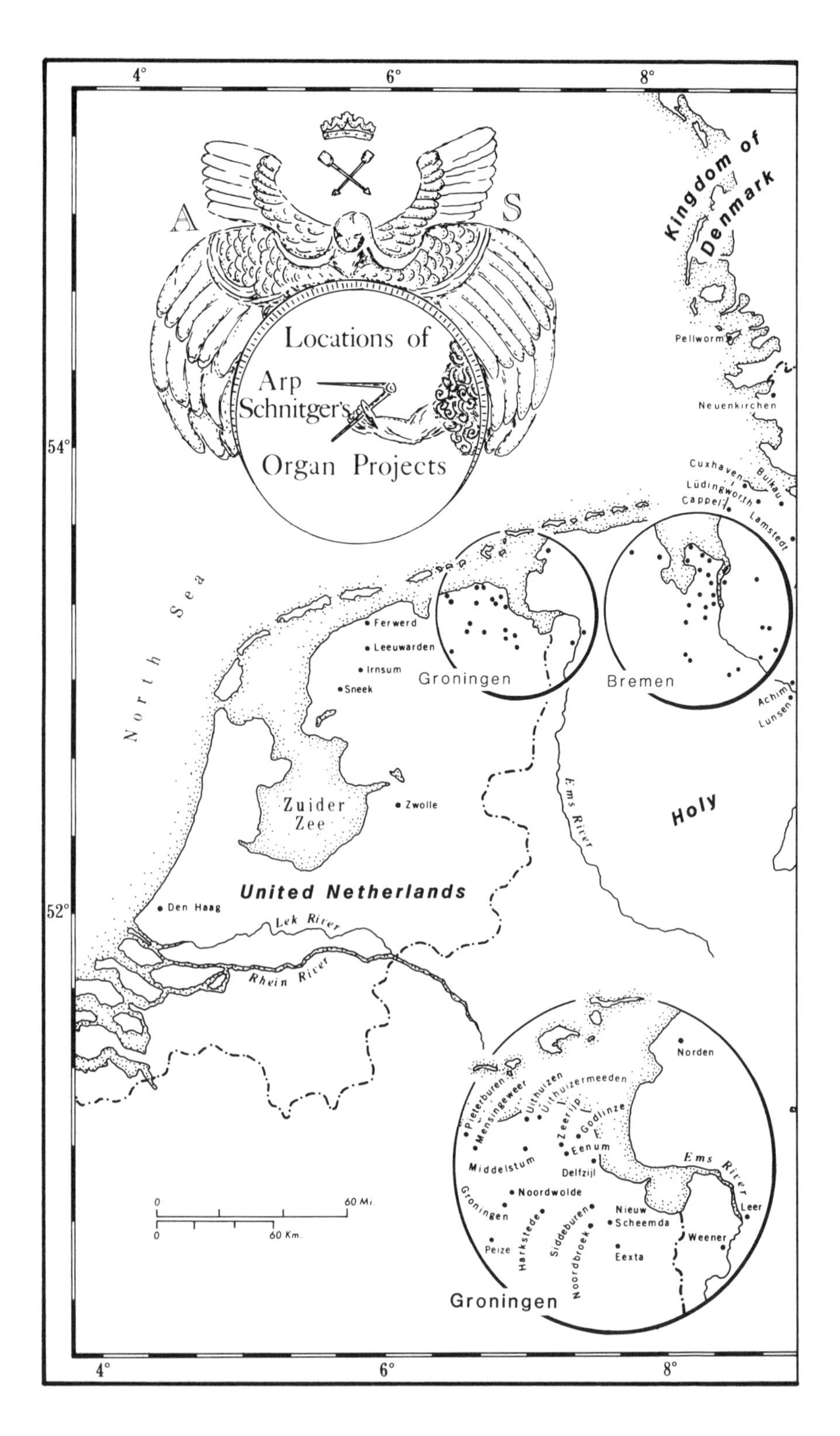

A S
Locations of
Arp
Schnitger's
Organ Projects
Kingdom of Denmark
Pellworm
Neuenkirchen
Cuxhaven
Bulkau
Lüdingworth
Cappel
Lamstedt
North Sea
Ferwerd
Leeuwarden
Irnsum
Sneek
Groningen
Bremen
Achim
Lunsen
Zuider Zee
Zwolle
Ems River
Holy
United Netherlands
Den Haag
Lek River
Rhein River
0
60 Mi.
0
60 Km.
Norden
Pieterburen
Mensingeweer
Uithuizen
Uithuizermeeden
Zeerijp
Godlinze
Eenum
Middelstum
Delfzijl
Noordwolde
Groningen
Harkstede
Siddeburen
Nieuw Scheemda
Noordbroek
Peize
Eexta
Weener
Leer
Ems River
Groningen
4°
6°
8°
54°
52°

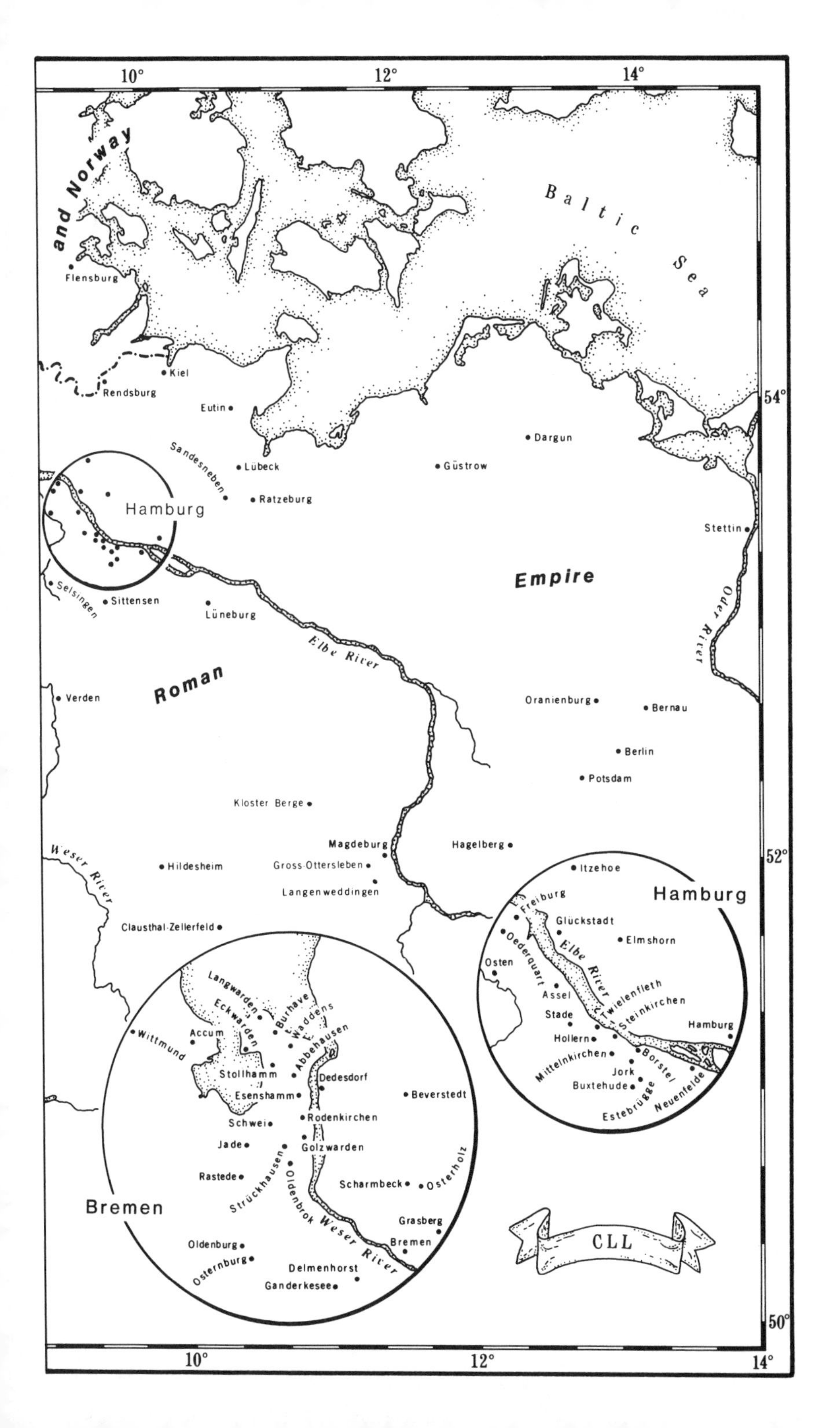
10°
12°
14°
and Norway
Baltic Sea
Flensburg
Kiel
Rendsburg
Eutin
Lübeck
Sandesneben
Ratzeburg
Güstrow
Dargun
Stettin
Oder River
Hamburg
Empire
Selsingen
Sittensen
Lüneburg
Elbe River
Roman
Verden
Oranienburg
Bernau
Berlin
Potsdam
Kloster Berge
Magdeburg
Hagelberg
Weser River
Hildesheim
Gross-Ottersleben
Langenweddingen
Clausthal-Zellerfeld
Itzehoe
Hamburg
Freiburg
Glückstadt
Elmshorn
Oederquart
Osten
Elbe River
Assel
Twielenfleth
Steinkirchen
Stade
Hamburg
Hollern
Mittelnkirchen
Borstel
Jork
Buxtehude
Estebrügge
Neuenfelde
Langwarden
Eckwarden
Burhave
Waddens
Abbehausen
Wittmund
Accum
Stollhamm
Dedesdorf
Esenshamm
Beverstedt
Rodenkirchen
Schwei
Jade
Golzwarden
Strückhausen
Oldenbrok
Rastede
Scharmbeck
Osterholz
Bremen
Grasberg
Weser River
Bremen
Oldenburg
Osternburg
Delmenhorst
Ganderkesee
CLL
54°
52°
50°

later on their German counterparts were preeminent in Holland. The names of Cornelius and Michael Slegal, Andreas and Marten de Mare, Edo Evers, Lampeler van Mill, and Johannes Millensis are scattered throughout the records of Oldenburg and Ostfriesland. The oldest evidence concerning both a builder and an organ in Ostfriesland was found on a choir organ on the Gospel side of the St. Maria Kirche in Marienhafe. It named one Thidericus de Dominis as having completed the instrument in 1437. The Patrozinium Kirche of nearby Rysum purchased a positiv in 1457 from a builder in Groningen, the Netherlands, possibly Johan ten Damme. Parts of this organ may still be extant, included in a 1513 organ documented by an inscription on the organ gallery. In 1927 it was determined that at least the four ranks of pipes marked with an asterisk were products of the early sixteenth century:[1]

*1.	Prinzipal	8′
*2.	Gedackt	8′
*3.	Oktave	4′
*4.	Oktave	2′
5.	Sesquialtera	2f.
6.	Mixtur	3–5f.
7.	Trompete	8′

Thus the exchange of talent was already in progress across the Ems River. Numerous mention is found between 1518 and 1538 in contract records of organ builders in Emden named Johannes: Johannes Molner; Johann, organ builder; Johann Bergherynnck; and Johannes Emedensis. The beautiful late Gothic (1526) organ Prospekt at Scheemda, now in the Rijksmuseum of Amsterdam, as well as a 1531 organ at Uphusen are attributed to the last-named. It is conceivable that all these builders were the same as "Emedensis," for one can hardly imagine Emden accommodating four reputable organ builders during the same twenty-year period!

The first major Netherlands builders to be recorded in

Germany were Cornelius and Michael Slegal, sons of the builder Georg Slegal of Zwolle. Their Ostfriesland work is noted in a listing submitted to the officials of St. Lamberti Kirche in Münster in the expectation of consideration as builders of a new organ there. Later their efforts extended to Westfalen, Bremen (Dom), Hildesheim (St. Andress), Stadthagen, Hoya, and Oldenburg. Most important of the Netherlands-German builders was the de Mare family, Andreas and sons Christoffer and Marten (Meerten), who supposedly left their home in Ghent because of the father's evangelical leanings and settled in Groningen, acquiring citizenship in 1560. Though the 1566-67 Andreas de Mare organ for the Ludgerikirche in Norden had a short life, it established this builder in Ostfriesland. In 1572 he was accorded the maintenance of the 1568 Koster organ in the Gross Kirche of Emden, work that occupied him for some ten years. The account books of this church hold multitudinous references to organ building, organ playing, and church music in general; and the vivid entries by the church's accountant give this portrait of the organ case:

> In the west part of the church, as counterpart to the Prince's Chair, on the balustrade there is a richly carved Renaissance Prospekt with three projecting Pedal towers, each crowned with three golden knobs; on each side of the Prospekt are placed winged doors whose surfaces are adorned with paintings by Hans von Coninxloo. The organ consists of Hauptwerk and Brustwerk with an independent Pedal.[2]

The plundering of the churches in the vicinity of Emden during the Spanish/Dutch battles drove de Mare inland. In 1583 he had begun work on a new organ for the Bremen Stephani-Kirche, utilizing there the design concept of the Emden Gross Kirche. Organs at the Marktkirche in Hannover (1589–94) and at the Kloister Kirche in Loccum (1594–99) marked his final opuses. Marten de Mare remained in Emden to care for the Gross Kirche organ, establishing himself as an independent builder. In 1595 he became a citizen of Bremen, where he completed organs for the church at Stellichte and for St. Ansgari. The cases of these organs, still preserved, are among the most-beautiful examples of Renaissance craftsmanship.

Edo Evers is considered along with the Netherlands builders, although his origins are not clear. To him fell the task of renovating de Mare's Norden organ (1616–18), the first instrument in the province to boast a Rückpositiv. His 1619 organ at St. Werenfridus in Osteel is preserved today with much of the original pipe work.

St. Werenfridus, Osteel[3]

Oberwerk			*Brustwerk*	
1. Prinzipal	8′	(Prospekt)	1. Hohlflöte	4′
2. Quintade	16′	(partly in Prospekt)	2. Spitzflöte	2′
3. Gedackt	8′		3. Sifflöte	1′
4. Oktave	4′		4. Regal	8′
5. Spitzflöte	4′			
6. Quinte	3′		Zimbelstern	
7. Oktave	2′		Tremulant	
8. Mixtur	4f.		3 Bellows	
9. Trompete	8′	(bass/descant)	Suspended Pedal	

[1885 report and repair estimate from Rohlfs]

Hamburg

Hamburg and its environs felt the influence of the Dutch following the Reformation, which temporarily drove the Brabant builders Gregorius Vogel, Hendrik Niehoff, and Jaspar Johansen to the more-peaceful Hanseatic locale. The leading native craftsmen were the Scherers: Jacob, who worked from about 1537 to 1574; Hans, the Elder, who carried the firm until about 1611; his son, Hans, the Younger, who was active until

1631; and Dirk Hoyer, Jacob's son-in-law, builder of the Steinkirchen organ in 1581. Closely associated with the Scherers was Hans Bockelmann, the Elder, head of the family of organ builders who worked out of Lüneburg from the late sixteenth century. He collaborated with Hans Scherer, the Elder, in 1592 on the rebuilding of the Hamburg Jacobikirche organ; and one year later he joined Antonius Wilde, famous for his Otterndorf organ, in building a new organ at Wöhrden.

Gottfried Fritzsche, the Saxon-electorate court organ builder, was responsible for maintaining the great Hamburg tradition through the Thirty Years' War and up to Schnitger's time. Driven by the war from Saxony via Braunschweig and Celle to Hamburg about 1630, he established a thriving business at Ottensen in the Hamburg area and trained Friedrich Stellwagen (Lübeck), his son-in-law; Jonas Weigl (Braunschweig); Tobias Brunner (Lunden); Franz Theodar Kretzschmar (Schwerin); Constantinus Ibach (Stade); and Joachim Appeldohrn (Hamburg). Fritzsche's influence was felt in Denmark and Sweden through the work of his son, Hans Christoph, and the latter's son-in-law, Hans Henric Cahman, known subsequently as the "Father of Swedish organ building." His art touched four major organists of his day, all pupils of Sweelinck, as Fritzsche rebuilt and enlarged the four major organs of Hamburg: St. Petri (Jacob Praetorius), St. Nikolai (Johann Praetorius), St. Katharinen (Heinrich Scheidemann), and St. Jacobi (Ulrich Cernitz), bringing the last two instruments to four manuals each. Surely he must also have had some influence on his stepson, the Pietist poet Johann Rist, called the "Nordic Apollo," who was the friend of many important musicians of his period. Among them were Heinrich Schütz, Christoph Bernhard, Andreas Hammerschmidt, and Scheidemann, all of whom collaborated with Rist on settings of his songs and hymns.

From these associations we have evidence of Hamburg's significance as a focal point of the arts during a period in which much of Europe was beset by confusion and unrest. The city was a magnet for instrument makers, many of whom established reputations far beyond the boundaries of their homeland. Foremost among them was the master violin and lute maker, Joachim Tielcke, whose creative period coincided with Schnitger's. In 1870 Friedrich Chrysander wrote of Hamburg's position at the close of the seventeenth century:

> In no free Reich-city, hardly even in a prince's court, had music such strong support as in Hamburg. In general it meant: the most meaningful, smartest and most excellent of poets, musicians and singers belonging to Germany were gathered in Hamburg. He who understood his profession most easily found there food and fame.[4]

Oldenburg

We owe much of our knowledge of the history of Baroque organ building in Oldenburg to descriptions made by Johann Wilhelm Krämershoff, the court organ builder, under stipulations made by the Oldenburg Consistory in 1802–1803. These specifications of 39 organs of the Oldenburg district and those of the Jever area given by the builder Johann Adam Berner c. 1760 offer the final comprehensive insight into the period preceding the almost wholesale destruction of old organs that occurred in the nineteenth century. It can be reasonably assumed that before the middle of the seventeenth century many of the small city churches and the ducal chapels possessed only a positiv organ. The important churches, such as St. Alexander in Wildeshausen and St. Lamberti in Oldenburg; the monastery churches at Rastede and Hude; and the wealthier "marshland" churches of Berne, Blexen, Hohenkirchen, Sengwarden, and Tettens invariably had an organ of greater magnitude.

From 1573 through the eighteenth century, organ building in Oldenburg enjoyed its most-fruitful period mainly because of Hammelmann's Church Edict and the ensuing emphasis on church visitations, which resulted in greater support for the art from both clergy and congregation.[5] Here, as in Ostfriesland and Hamburg, the influence of the Netherlands builders was strongly felt. The encouragement given organ builders by the ruling royalty was a third important growth factor, spurred on by the constant competition between the duchies of Delmenhorst (under Anton II, died 1619, and later Christian, died 1647) and Oldenburg (under Anton Günther II, 1603–67). It was Count Anton II who contracted with Christian Bockelmann in 1618 for the Delmenhorst St. Maria organ, later rebuilt by Schnitger (1707). Christian, of the Lüneberg Bockelmann family, carried out the rebuilding of the Stephani and Martini Kirche organs of Bremen between 1615 and 1618 and maintained the Lüneburg city organ between 1601 and 1629.

The Sieburgs, another Lower Saxony family, were driven by the war to Bremen in 1624. (In 1617–20 they had built a twenty-stop organ for the Göttingen Jacobi Kirche.) The father, Johann Sieburg, came under the patronage of Count Christian and was later named his "Organ and Instrument Maker." Yet he did not have enough influence to wrest the Oldenburg Lamberti Kirche contract from Gerd Kröger. The resultant rivalry between their families was similar to the Schnitger–Kayser competition, which was to arise fifty years later. Jodocus (Jost) Sieburg, the son, carried the family tradition into new works at Riepe (1641–42), Westerhusen (1642–43), the Aurich Schlosskapelle (1642), and St. Georg at Sengwarden (1644), the specifications of which were reported by Johann Lübben of Jever in 1709. With the exception of the Pedal tower in Berne, the Sengwarden Prospekt is the oldest in the province of Oldenburg.

Count Anton Günther and the organist Hermannus Cropp, who succeeded to the post at St. Lamberti in Oldenburg in 1632, may be credited with drawing the Kröger family to Oldenburg. This family was responsible for the sophistica-

St. Georg, Sengwarden[6]

Oberwerk

1.	Prinzipal	8′
2.	Gedackt	8′
3.	Oktave	4′
4.	Quinta	3′
5.	Oktave	2′
6.	Mixtur	4f.
7.	Trompete	8′

Rückpositiv

1.	Prinzipal	4′
2.	Quintadena	8′
3.	Spitzflöte	4′

Rückpositiv (cont.)

4.	Quinta	1⅓′
5.	Zimbel	2f.
6.	Schalmei	

Pedal

1.	Quintadena	16′
2.	Oktave	4′
3.	Trompete	8′

Tremulant

tion of the organ-building art immediately preceding Huss and Schnitger. In 1634, the marriage of the count gave impetus to plans dating from 1607 for the rebuilding of the Slegel organ in St. Lamberti; and Cropp, who called himself "Begensis," influenced Anton to summon Gerd Kröger from Westphalia, where he was working in the Duchy of Ravensberg. The specifications of the Lamberti organ have not been preserved; it is only known that it was a three-manual instrument with Pedal towers, mounted on spring-chests, the method of building chests that Kröger brought from Westphalia. Gerd died some time before 1642, and the completion of the organ was left to Hermann (either his brother or his son—the records are unclear). The organ which held its position as the largest instrument in Northwest Germany until Schnitger completed the Norden Ludgerikirche organ in 1688, stimulated organ building and established the image of the "Oldenburger" organ.

Hermann was probably the builder of the Langwarden organ in 1650, assisted by Berendt Huss. The instrument has the earmarks of the Kröger spring-chests and Pedal towers placed on both sides of the Oberwerk/Brustwerk. Finding no challenge after these enterprises, in November 1651 Hermann contracted for the building of the Celle Stadtkirche organ. The preservation of this Prospekt at Celle gives an idea of the probable appearance of the Lamberti organ. Another move took Kröger and his family of two daughters to Nienburg in 1655, from which his business grew rapidly. The work list included new organs for Bücken (1655), Nendorf (1656), Mariendrebber (1659), and Hoya (1660), as well as repairs to the de Mare organ in the Verden Dom (1660), at St. Ansgari in Bremen, and to the Nienburg town church (1670).

Following the death of Kröger, Berendt Huss, who had worked with him as master apprentice on the construction of the Celle Stadtkirche organ, became the connecting link to Arp Schnitger. His marriage on April 23, 1654 at St. Lamberti in Oldenburg, records of tax payments there between 1654 and 1658, and the baptism of his son Gottfried on March 4, 1656 document his whereabouts after leaving Celle. In 1660 Huss built an organ at Eckwarden for the St. Martin Kirche, where his son Elias Otto became organist in 1688. Not finding sufficient work in Oldenburg, Huss was also active in Holstein and Stade; and in 1663 he purchased a house in Glückstadt, where he had moved earlier. The contract for the Glückstadt organ, signed in 1661, spelled the beginning of years of debt and worry. The organ was scheduled for completion by Christmas of 1663, but delays forced Huss to seek a loan for materials in October 1664 and again in 1665. A choir organ for St. Lamberti in 1668 and major repair of Kröger's Lamberti organ in 1667–70, in which his apprentice, Arp Schnitger, participated, were among Huss's final contributions to Schnitger's inheritance.

2. Organ at Patrozinium Kirche, Rysum, 1513.

3. Prospekt of the organ at Scheemda. Johannes Emedensis, 1526. Now in Rijksmuseum, Amsterdam.

St. Werenfridus, Osteel. 4. Exterior of the church. 5. Prospekt. Edo Evers, 1619. *Opposite: Upper left,* 6. Detail of Prospekt with Prinzipal 8′. *Upper right,* 7. Quintade 16′ from inside Prospekt. *Lower left,* 8. Brustwerk. *Lower right,* 9. Hohlflöte 4′, Spitzflöte 2′, Sifflöte 1′.

EHRE SEI GOT

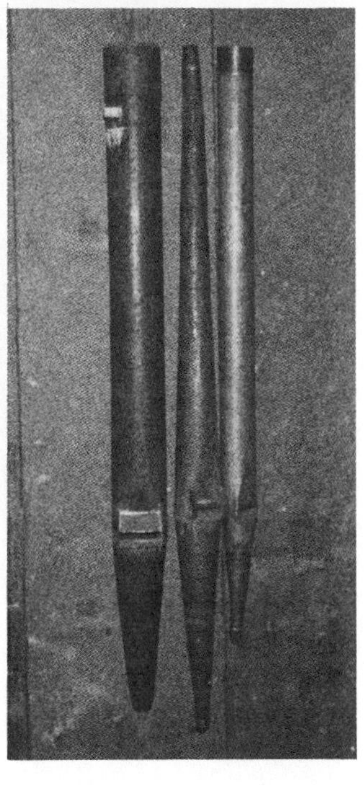

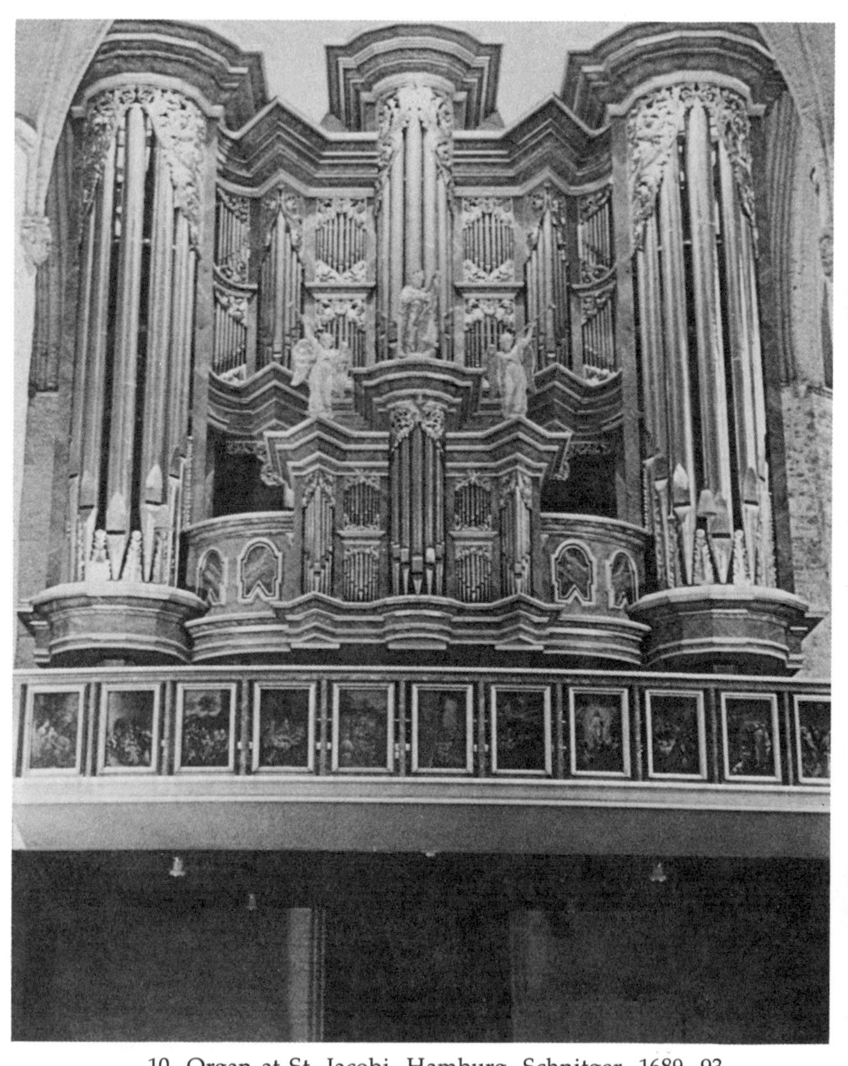

10. Organ at St. Jacobi, Hamburg. Schnitger, 1689–93.

11. Organ at St. Georg, Sengwarden.
Jodocus (Jost) Sieburg, 1644.

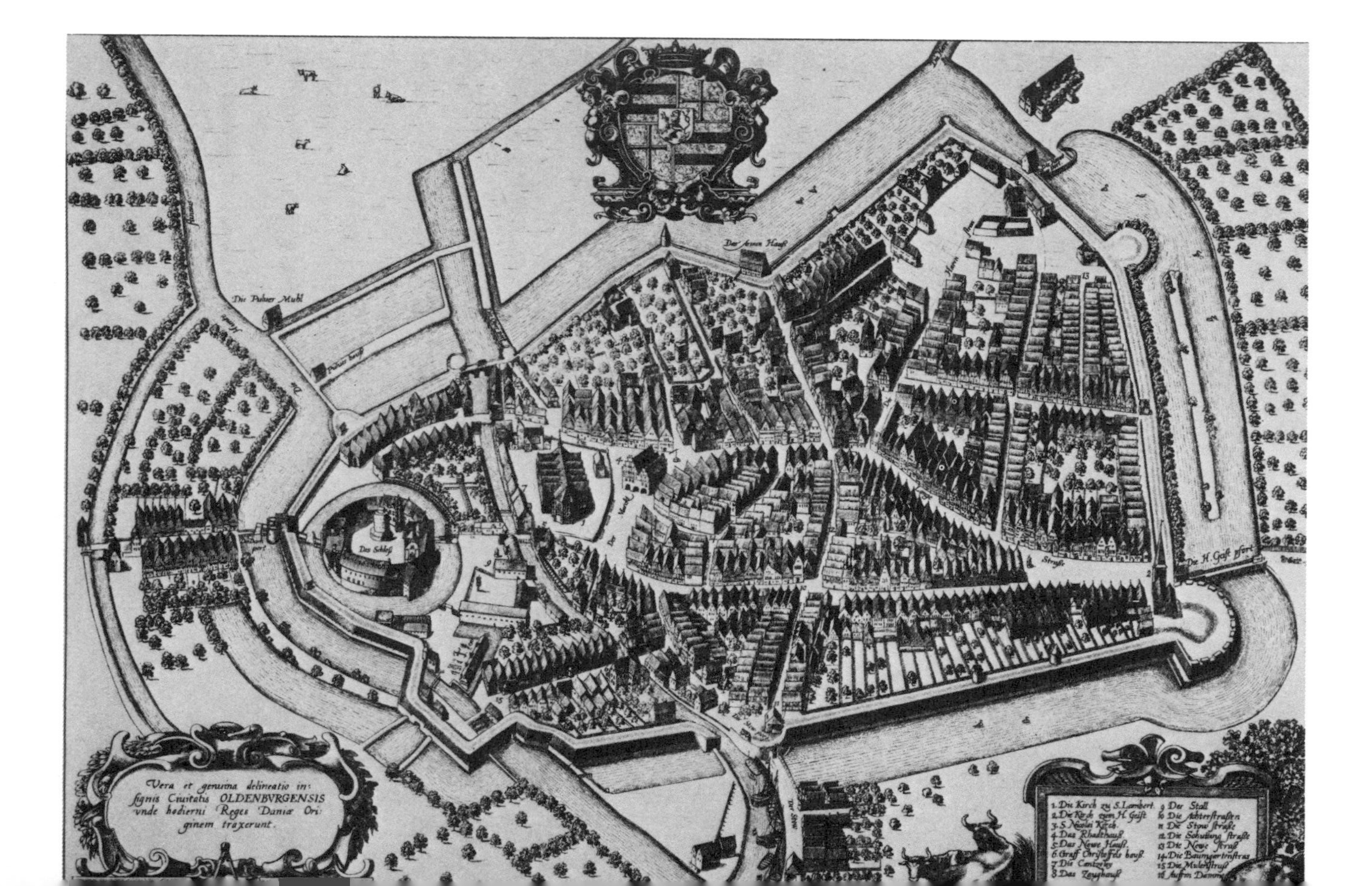
Vera et genuina delineatio in:
signis Ciuitatis OLDENBVRGENSIS
vnde hodierni Reges Daniæ Ori:
ginem traxerunt.
1. Die Kirch zu S. Lambert.
2. Die Kirch zum H. Geist
3. S. Nicolai Kirch.
4. Das Rhadthauß
5. Das Newe Hauß.
6. Graff Christoffels hauß.
7. Die Cantzley
8. Das Zeughauß
9 Der Stall
10 Die Achterstraßen
11 Die Stow straße
12 Die Schuttung straße
13 Die Newe straß
14 Die Baumgertenstraß
15 Die Mulenstraß
Das Schloß
Die Pulver Muhl
Der Armen Hauß
Die H. Geist pfort

Opposite: 12. Seventeenth-century map of the city of Oldenburg.

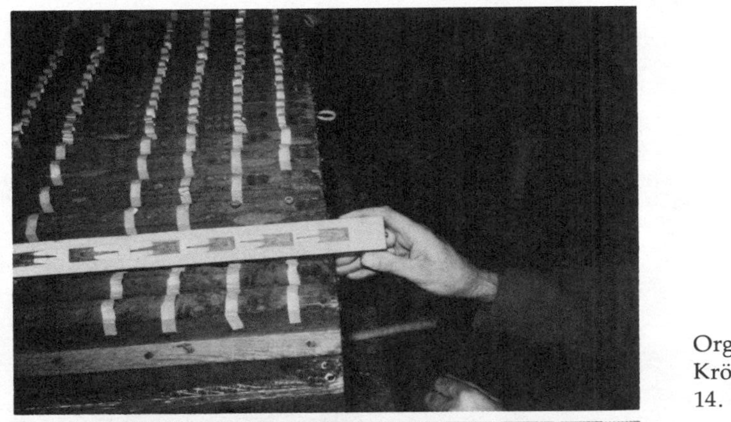

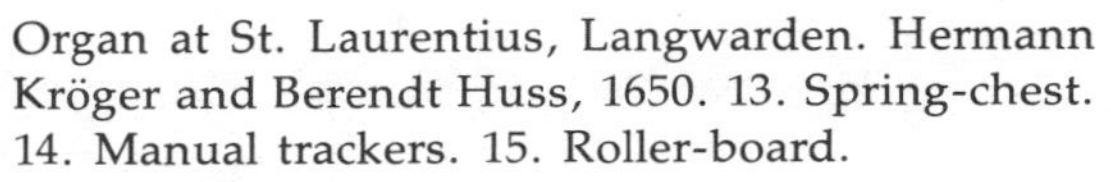

Organ at St. Laurentius, Langwarden. Hermann Kröger and Berendt Huss, 1650. 13. Spring-chest. 14. Manual trackers. 15. Roller-board.

16. Organ Prospekt at St. Laurentius, Langwarden.

An institution is the lengthened shadow of one man.
—RALPH WALDO EMERSON

2. Measure of the Man

ARP Schnitger is considered by many organ historians to have been the master builder of the Baroque. He was born into his profession on July 2, 1648 in Schmalenfleth near Golzwarden in Oldenburg, North Germany. Preceded by generations of Schnitger carpenters, joiners, cabinetmakers, and wood carvers, he served from c.1660 to 1666 as a joinery apprentice with his father, who was well known locally for his exquisite carvings on organ cases. At 18 Schnitger was apprenticed to his cousin Berendt Huss, and during the period 1668–76 he was actively involved in the building of the organ for St. Cosmae in Stade, residing in Stade throughout the project. Huss died in 1676, and Schnitger remained in Stade for six more years, completing the St. Wilhadi organ, begun by Huss (it was destroyed by lightning in 1724), and repairing the St. Nikolai instrument. Other contracts fulfilled for Huss's estate were repairs to organs in Freiburg/Niederelbe, Borstel/Altes Land, Himmelpforten, Assel/Kehdingen, and Jork/Altes Land; a new one-division organ built in 1678 for Scharmbeck (near Bremen), parts of which survive in the Erasmus Bielfeldt organ, built in 1731–34; and a two-division plus Pedal instrument for Bülkau/Niederelbe, completed in 1679.

Schnitger's first contract as an independent builder came in 1678, when he undertook a three-division plus Pedal, 28-stop instrument for Oederquart/Niederelbe. It was completed on September 10, 1682.

In 1679 and 1680 Schnitger was also building a two-

ST. JOHANNIS, OEDERQUART[1]

Hauptwerk	
Principal	8′
Quintadena	16′
Gedact	8′
Octave	4′
Gedact	4′
Nasat	3′
Octave	2′
Gemshorn	2′
Quinte	1½′
Rauschpfeife	2f.
Mixtur	4–5f.
Trompete	8′
Brustwerk	
Gedact	4′
Octave	2′
Regal	8′
Rückpositiv	
Principal	4′
Gedact	8′
Rückpositiv (cont.)	
Octave	2′
Sesquialtera	2f.
Mixtur	4f.
Dulcian	8′
Schalmey	4′
Pedal	
Principal	8′
Subbass	16′
Octave	4′
Posaune	16′
Trompete	8′
Trompete	4′

Pedal-coupler
Tremulant
Zimbelstern
Bell-stop
6 Bellows

division plus Pedal, 30-register organ for St. Johannis-Kloster in Hamburg. This organ was moved to Cappel near Bremerhaven in 1816 and is in use there today at St. Petri und St. Pauli. Though the organs of Oederquart and Cappel have a similar number of stops, much more attention was devoted to the independence of the Pedal in the latter, and the prominence of its mixtures is obvious.

1680–1689

The years 1680 and 1681 came and went with the disappointment of unrealized negotiations on a rebuild in Lüdingworth/Cuxhaven, repairs in Hamburg-Kerchwerder, and a

St. Petri und St. Pauli, Cappel[2]

Hauptwerk (Manual II)

S	Prinzipal	8′
O	Quintadena	16′
O	Hollfloit	8′
O	Oktave	4′
S	Spitzfloit	4′
S	Rauschpfeife	2f.
O	Nasat	2⅔′
O	Gemshorn	2′
S	Mixtur	5–6f.
S	Zimbel	3f.
O	Trompete	8′

Rückpositiv (Manual I)

S	Prinzipal	4′
O	Gedackt	8′
S	Quintadena	8′
S	Sesquialtera	2f.
S	Floit	4′
S	Oktave	2′
S	Terzian	2f.

Rückpositiv (cont.)

S	Siffloit	1⅓′
S	Scharff	4–6f.
S	Dulzian	16′

Pedal

O	Untersatz	16′
O	Oktave	8′
S	Oktave	4′
S	Nachthorn	2′
S	Rauschpfeife	2′
S	Mixtur	4–6f.
S	Posaune	16′
S	Trompete	4′
	Cornet	2′

Manual Couplers
Tremulant
Zimbelstern
Wind pressure: 72mm
Pitch: nearly ½ tone above normal (g♯′ = 435Hz)

S: existing stops built by Schnitger
O: stops retained from a sixteenth-century organ

report for the Pfarrkirche in Güstrow consuming much of Schnitger's time. In 1682 Schnitger established himself as an organ builder in Hamburg, and in July of that year the contract for the Lüdingworth rebuild was finally signed. That organ is extant and retains the Schnitger chests in the Hauptwerk, Rückpositiv, and Pedal; a Schnitger 2-rank Rauschpfeife in the Hauptwerk; a Schnitger Rückpositiv complete except for part of the Prinzipal 4′ and the Vox Humana 8′; and a Schnitger 3-rank Scharf in the Pedal, as well as the Pedal tower Prinzipal

8′. Most of the other ranks date from Antonius Wilde in 1598–99. The large four-division, 67-stop organ for St. Nikolai in Hamburg was begun in 1682 and took five years to build. It was destroyed by fire in 1842, a fate that was also to befall the organs of St. Pauli (built 1687), St. Petri (built 1692), St. Gertrudis (built 1699–1700), and St. Michaelis (built 1712–15) in Hamburg; St. Stephani (built 1695–98) in Bremen; and Neuenkirchen (built 1705) in Dithmarschen.

Altes Land, the district between Stade and Hamburg, is the area most closely associated with the life and work of Arp Schnitger. His marriage, the church that offered his first opportunity to build a new organ in Altes Land, the workshop that was to train so many fine craftsmen—all were centered in Neuenfelde, a small town between Buxtehude and Harburg. Schnitger's building activity eventually involved eight of the ten churches in the area: four new organs (Neuenfelde, Steinkirchen, Hollern, and Estebrügge) and four renovations (Jork, Borstel, Twielenfleth, and Mittelnkirchen).

The contract for the Neuenfelde organ was signed in February 1682, though work on the instrument was not to commence until 1687. The next year, 1683, was another one of estimates and rebuilds, but in 1684 Schnitger built three two-manual-plus-Pedal organs in Oldenburg, Ostfriesland, and Holstein. His marriage to Gertrud Otte of Neuenfelde took place on February 3, 1684, and part of her dowry in Neuenfelde became his "Orgelbauerhof." Today this house bears a plaque reading:

Hof des Orgelbauers
ARP SCHNITGER
1648–1719

The Schnitgers' first child, Agneta, was born on February 5, 1685 and lived only seven months. Their four sons—Arp, Hans, Johann Jürgen, and Franz Caspar—were born in 1686,

1688, 1690, and 1693 respectively, and all became organ builders in their own right. Another daughter, Catharina, was born in November 1697.

In 1684 a rivalry arose between Schnitger and Joachim Kayser over the jealously guarded rights and privileges of organ building in Oldenburg, Jeverland, and Ostfriesland. This infamous conflict started over the issue of a contract with the parish in Wittmund/Ostfriesland, which had contracted with Kayser on July 23, 1684 for the rebuilding of its organ. Schnitger was then working on a new instrument at St. Secundus in Schwei/Oldenburg, and very naturally he may have extended himself in an effort to make inroads into Ostfriesland. At the beginning of September 1684, scarcely one month after having signed with Kayser, the Wittmund parish also signed a contract with Schnitger for a new organ (with two manuals and a free-standing Pedal, which he built that year) and attempted to dissolve Kayser's contract. The leading force in this action was most likely Pastor Engelbert Bronner (Brümmer), who was born in 1641 in Groden, served for a time as organist in Neuenkirchen/Hadeln, and was pastor in Otterndorf from 1669 to 1681. Exposed to Schnitger's instruments under construction, Bronner influenced the congregation to negotiate with the famed builder. Also influential in the capitulation was the Wittmund organist, Johannes Angelbeck, who hailed from the Stade area and knew Schnitger's work there. The ensuing suit brought by Kayser against the parish dragged on from 1685 until 1692. In the meantime, Kayser generally maintained his hold in Ostfriesland and Jever, building perhaps his two finest organs, those at St. Stephan/Schortens (1686) and at St. Sixtus/Hohenkirchen (1694–99).

Undoubtedly the Schnitger organ that is tonally best preserved is the one in Steinkirchen, which was begun in 1685 and completed in 1687. It stands in a small, unobtrusive church near the Elbe River surrounded by decaying tombstones. St. Ludgeri in Norden/Ostfriesland, 1687–88, provides us with an unusual example of congregational interest in an organ project. During the actual course of construction the organ was enlarged from the initial contract. It is one of the largest (III+P/46) of Schnitger's surviving instruments, and boasts some of the loveliest mutations imaginable. The organ is situated midway of the nave on a balcony and is equally audible throughout the church.

In 1687 work began on the Hamburg-Neuenfelde organ, for which Schnitger had signed a contract in 1682. This church marks the final resting place for the master; and the organ, which stands as Schnitger's memorial, is once again worthy of his name following Paul Ott's 1980 restoration. The St. Cosmae organ in Stade (renovated in 1975 and long famous for its still-functioning, double spring-chests in the Hauptwerk) again occupied Schnitger when he was commissioned in 1688 by Vincent Lübeck to make significant changes in Huss's specifications. Interestingly enough, four of Schnitger's extant organs were constructed during 1687–88.

In 1687 the paths of two of the Baroque's most important musical figures crossed. In May Dietrich Buxtehude traveled to Hamburg to inspect the nearly completed Schnitger organ at St. Nikolai. Buxtehude's great organ at the Marienkirche in Lübeck (built in the sixteenth century by M. Barthold) had exhibited numerous defects as early as 1671, and the repairs of Joachim Richborn (1673), Balthasar Held (1685), and Johann Nette (1686) served only as stopgap measures. Buxtehude was authorized by the church officials to examine Schnitger's work, and he reported that it had been "manufactured with good success and manifold pleasure" and that he had tested it and "found it to his good satisfaction."[3] As is frequently the case, the church officials failed to act on their organist's recommendation that Schnitger be commissioned with a "correction" of the Marienkirche organ, and in 1688 an itinerant Dresden organ repairman remedied only the major defects of the instrument. Nor did a definite commission result from

Schnitger's personal visit to Lübeck in the spring of 1689, for which he received 24 M. for expenses. Thus it was that the Marienkirche organ continued in a state of disrepair even after the completion of Schnitger's marvelous organ in the Lübeck Dom in 1698.

1690–1699

The fame of Schnitger was spreading. In 1690 he built a small organ for export to England, followed in 1691 by a 16-register instrument for the Grand Duke in Moscow, who was later to become Czar Peter the Great. Numerous house organs left Schnitger's hands between 1690 and 1712, ranging from a II/16 for Pastor Dr. Hinckelmann in Bremen to a I/6 for Prince von Sönder in Hagelberg/Brandenburg and a I/6 Positiv for the Collegium Musicum in Groningen.

COLLEGIUM MUSICUM[4]

Holpijp	8′	Sexquialter	2st.
Fluit doux	4′	Mixtur	4st.
Quint	3′	Vox Humana disc.	8′
Praestant	2′		

Schnitger's first contract for the Netherlands involved a comprehensive rebuild of the Martinikerk in Groningen. The original one-manual organ had been built in 1479 under the supervision of the famed Rudolf Agricola, Renaissance organ builder, humanist, and city secretary, and incorporated as the Rugwerk in Andreas de Mare's large 1542 instrument. Both the principal and flute choruses were well developed in the Agricola opus and were retained by Schnitger in 1691. The present Martinikerk organ includes pipe work from five centuries and boasts a Praestant 32′, the only preserved 32′ stop built by Schnitger.[5]

Martinikerk, Groningen

Hoofdwerk (Manual II)

Praestant 16′, 1542; from g', 1854
Octaaf 8′, 1542
Roerfluit 8′, 1854
Quintadena 8′, 1627
Wilgenpijp 8′, 1854
Superoctaaf 4′, 1729
Speelfluit 4′, 1627
Quinte 2⅔′, 1845, cone-shaped
Flageolet 2′, 1854
Cornet 5 ranks, 1808 and 1854, in treble from c'
Mixtuur 4–5 ranks, 1854
Fagot 16′, 1939, cylindrical
Trompet 8′, 1691
Vox humana 8′, 1939

Rugpositief (Manual I)

Quintadena 16′, before 1542; original Praestant 8′ from c°
Praestant 8′, 1740
Wijdgedekt 8′, before 1542; from c''', conical, open
Roerfluit 8′, 1729
Octaaf 4′, 1854
Fluit 4′, 1542 (C-B) and 1816; from f♯'', conical, open
Superoctaaf 2′, 1729
Holfluit 2′, before 1542; C-B, stopped; c-f♯', conical, open; remainder, cylindrical, open
Quint 1⅓′, 1729; C-B, stopped
Sifflet 1′, 1816
Sesquialtera 2 ranks, 1939, treble
Mixtuur 3–4 ranks, 1854; from c', 1939
Tertscymbel 3 ranks, 1939
Trompet 8′, 1939

Rugpositief (cont.)

Ranket 8′, 1939
Schalmei 4′, 1939

Bovenwerk (Manual III)

Praestant 8′ 1–3 ranks, 1542; from c°, 2 ranks; from c', 3 ranks
Holpijp 8′, 1854, C-B, wood
Open Nachthorn 8′, 1542; c°-f♯°, stopped; remainder open
Viola da Gamba 8′, 1816
Octaaf 4′, 1542
Open Fluit 4′, 1854, cylindrical
Woudfluit 2′, 1808; C-B, stopped; remainder, cylindrical, open
Scherp 4–6 ranks, 1939
Kromhoorn 8′, 1939

Pedaal

Praestant 32′, 1691; C-E, stopped, wood; from F, open
Principaal 16′, 1542, C-F, wood
Subbas 16′, 1854
Octaafbas 8′, 1542
Bourdon 8′, 1740
Octaaf 4′, 1542
Roerfluit 2′, 1740
Quinte 1⅓′, 1816
Ruischpijp 3 ranks, 1939
Bombarde 32′, 1939
Bazuin 16′, 1691
Trompet 8′, 1691
Klaroen 4′, 1691
Cinck 2′, 1939

2 Tremulants
8 Bellows
Wind pressure: 75 mm
Pitch: normal

1479 Rudolph Agricola (oldest known specifications)
1542 Andreas de Mare
1627 Antonius and Adam Verbeeck
1691 Arp Schnitger
1729 Franz Caspar Schnitger
1740 Albert Antonius Hinsch
1808 and 1816 Nicolaus Albertus Lohman
1854 Petrus van Oeckelen
1939 J. de Koff

Magdeburg provided Schnitger with an abundance of work, since the city had been virtually destroyed during the Thirty Years' War. His second largest organ was built there for St. Johannis (1689–94); and though it is not extant the disposition is important to our overview. The preponderance of mixtures, the 16′ manual registers, and the comprehensive Pedal reed chorus are all noteworthy.

Also a visual work of art, the organ boasted a console and key frames inlaid with ivory and ebony and naturals covered with very thick ivory. Since such a large instrument required inventiveness in winding, it seems safe to assume that Schnitger consulted his friend Otto von Guericke, burgomeister of Magdeburg and inventor of the air pump, regarding air pressure and methods of supplying air.

Schnitger's reputation was fast becoming established in the Netherlands. In 1694–97 the Groningen Aa-Kerk organ (IV+P/40) was built, the largest of the Dutch organs actually completed by the master. Tragically, the organ collapsed on April 12, 1710, when the church towers caved in. Although Schnitger was requested in 1717 to build a new instrument utilizing portions of his previous opus, the project was not undertaken, probably because of his failing health. Schnitger contributed posthumously to the Aa-Kerk, however, for in 1814–15 King Willem I had the 1700–1702 Schnitger organ moved there from the Academie-or-Broerkerk. Today, some of Schnitger's work remains, including the Prospekt pipes, as well as a number of registers attributed to de Mare.

St. Johannis, Magdeburg[6]

Hauptwerk (Manual II)		*Oberpositiv* (Manual I)	
Principal, English tin	16′	Principal, English tin	8′
Qvintadeen	16′	Bordun	16′
Rohr-Flöthe	16′	Rohr-Flöthe	8′
Octava	8′	Qvintadeen	8′
Spitzflöthe	8′	Grobgedackt	8′
Gedackt	8′	Viol d'Gamba	8′
Qvinta	6′	Octava	4′
Octava	4′	Spitzflöthe	4′
Rohrflöthe	4′	Waltflöthe	2′
Koppel-Flöthe	4′	Qvintflöthe	1½′
Super Octava	2′	Siflöthe	1′
Flach-Flöthe	2′	Sesqvialtera	2f.
Rauschpfeife	3f.	Scharff	5, 6, 7f.
Mixtur	6, 7, 8f.	Trechter Regal	8′
Trompet	16′	Vox Humana	8′
Dulcian	8′	Schalmey	4′

Brustpositiv (Manual III)		*Pedal*	
Principal, English tin	8′	Principal, English tin	16′
Holtz-Flöthen	8′	Subbass	16′
Octava	4′	Octava	8′
Block Flöthen	4′	Gembs Horn	8′
Nassat	3′	Octava	4′
Octava	2′	Flöthe	4′
Gembs Horn	2′	Nachthorn	2′
Tertian	2f.	Rauschpfeiffe	3f.
Scharff	4, 5, 6f.	Mixtur	6, 7, 8f.
Cimbel	3f.	Posaune	32′
Dulcian	16′	Posaune	16′
Trompet	8′	Dulcian	16′
Trompet	4′	Trompet	8′
		Trompet	4′
		Cornet	2′

2 Tremulants
12 Bellows, 10′ × 5′
2 Zimbelstern

Aa-Kerk, Groningen[7]

Manuaal (Hoofdwerk)

1.	Praestant	16′
2.	Octaaf	8′
3.	Roerfluit	8′
4.	Octaaf	4′
5.	Holfluit	4′
6.	Ruispijp	2st.
7.	Supraoctaaf	2′
8.	Mixtuur	6–8st.

Borstwerk

[disposition unknown]

Bovenwerk

1.	Praestant	8′
2.	Holpijp	8′
3.	Salicet	8′
4.	Octaaf	4′
5.	Nasaet	3′
6.	Sesquialtera	2st.
7.	Mixtuur	4–6st.
8.	Trompet	8′
9.	Vox Humana	8′

Rugwerk

1.	Praestant	8′
2.	Gedekt	8′
3.	Quintadena	8′
4.	Octaaf	4′
5.	Woudfluit	2′
6.	Quint	1½′
7.	Sesquialtera	2st.
8.	Mixtuur	4–6st.
9.	Dulciaan	8′

Pedaal

1.	Praestant	16′
2.	Octaaf	8′
3.	Octaaf	4′
4.	Mixtuur	4–6st.
5.	Bazuin	16′
6.	Trompet	8′
7.	Schalmei	4′
8.	Cornet	2′

2 Tremulants
8 Bellows

Between the Aa-Kerk construction and 1700 Schnitger built twelve organs for the Netherlands, including the Noordbroek Hervormde Kerk organ (II+P/20), of which there are eleven and a half Schnitger registers extant, and the 1695–96 Positiv for the Nieuw Scheemda Hervormde Kerk (I/8), which is the only Schnitger remaining with its original unequal temperament. The specifications were given by Bernhardt H. Edskes in 1968, when the Positiv was restored by Metzler & Söhne of Zürich under his supervision.

Hervormde Kerk, Nieuw Scheemda[8]

1. Praestant 4′:	C–b°, Freytag (in Prospekt) c′–c″, Schnitger c♯″–c‴, Reconstruction
2. Holpijp 8′:	Schnitger (only the beards and feet were repaired)
3. Quint 3′:	C–b°, Schnitger (pipe feet and edges repaired) c′–c‴, Schnitger material (following the 1810 rebuild by N. A. Lohman, Groningen, these were in the Quintadena 4′)
4. Octaaf 2′:	Schnitger
5. Fluit 4′:	c′–c″, Schnitger (feet and beards repaired) C–b°, Reconstruction
6. Quintadena 8′: (descant)	New
7. Mixtuur III st.: (½′)	Reconstruction
8. Trompet 8′:	Copied from the Schnitger organ at Eenum, Groningen
Tremulant:	Constructed similarly to that at Dedesdorf

Another historically important small organ was built in 1696 for the Hervormde Kerk at Pieterburen. The contract of March 28, 1696 called for the following registers:[9]

1. Praestant	8′	[of pure tin; C D E to speak with the Gedekt]
2. Gedekt	8′	
3. Octave	4′	
4. Quinte	3′	
5. Supra Octav	2′	
6. Sexquialter	2st.	[The last three registers were to be halved
7. Mixtuir	3, 4, 5st.	so as to be playable separately in the bass
8. Cromphorn	8′	and treble.]

45 Keys: C D E F G A–c‴
Tremulant
3 Bellows, 5′ long × 3′ wide

However, Schnitger built a Trompete 8′ rather than the Cromphorn. His payment for the organ was 550 Gulden, 50

Gulden less than was paid to Allert Meijer, the builder of the organ case and gallery. Meijer constructed a Rugpositief facade in 1701; and 1704 brought the addition of a pull-down Pedal by Johan Radeker (Ratje), a Schnitger journeyman. Albert Antonius Hinsch (who married Franz Caspar Schnitger's widow) rebuilt the organ in 1772, supplying a new wind-chest to accommodate a 49-note manual, adding a Fluit 4′ as the ninth register and releathering the bellows. In 1867 H.S.G. Lohman of Assen replaced the Sesquialtera and Mixtuir with a Salicional 8′ and Viola di Gamba 8′ (Treble); and in 1901 the organ was moved to the Hervormde Kerk in Mensingeweer. The false Rugpositief and Meijer balustrade have remained at Pieterburen, where they frame a 1901 organ built by Friedrich Leichel of Lochem.

The building in 1696–98 of the beautiful ornate organ for the Dom in Lübeck (III+P/45)[10] marks a major contribution by one of Schnitger's numerous pupils, or journeymen.[11] A resident of Lübeck, Hans Hantelmann was the logical choice to carry out the work at the Dom. His previous experience under Schnitger included the St. Johannis organ in Magdeburg. Simultaneous with the Lübeck Dom project were a 1697 house organ for Herr Ernhorn in Moscow; estimates for Golzwarden/Oldenburg and Dedesdorf (near Bremerhaven); acceptance of organs for Bremen's Dom and St. Stephani; and in 1698, completion of organs for Golzwarden (II+P/20), Dedesdorf (II/12), and Strückhausen (II/12). One marvels at the mind and organizational powers of Schnitger, that he could, within the terms of the contract, meet the logistical problems and stipulations set forth for this twelve-voice instrument while simultaneously overseeing the building of the Lübeck Dom organ, especially in a period of history when communication was very difficult.

Schnitger's hometown, Golzwarden, the neighboring town of Schwei, Neuenfelde, and Oldenburg were the most frequent recipients of his altruism. In 1695 the report of the official inspection of the Golzwarden organ read:

> It is highly necessary that this organ, which has already been very rickety for several years—the bellows ripped, the wind channels completely stopped up so that almost no tuning will hold—should be repaired unless it is to remain *completely* silent. In this connection it is to be remembered that the famous organ builder, Arp Schnitger, who built the expensive organ in Hamburg [St. Nikolai], as well as being in the process of building a new organ in the Thumbskirche [Dom] in Bremen, has voluntarily offered, because he was born in this parish, to repair and make it playable; so everyone should have cause to thank him for this, since, to the honor of God and this parish, he does not ask more than the cost of materials and his food, which the parish must furnish. Whereby he then reminds that it must be decided now because he is working in Bremen. Once he has left there, he would hardly have time to take on this work.[12]

On May 9, 1697 Schnitger gave the church council an affidavit in which he outlined the necessary work to be accomplished:

> the removal of the bellows from the bellows chamber outside the church to the floor of the church and thorough repair thereof;
> rebuilding of the Hauptwerk chamber;
> replacement of both manual keyboards (compass C–a^2) with the extension to C, D, E in the great octave;
> replacement of the pedalboard as well as the addition of a Posaune 16′ in the Pedal.[13]

The cost was to be 245 Rtl. One year later the parish decided to move the organ to a platform to be built in the west end of the church, necessitating a new organ case and a new Prospekt. An almost totally new instrument resulted, according to the parish records of 1700. From Schnitger's point of view, the added work amounted to an additional 135 Rtl., his actual expense. It must be noted, however, that the labor actually fell mainly to Schnitger's journeymen, Johann Hinrich Ulenkampf and Johann Mattias Naumann. In October 1698 they received a tip of 4 Rtl![14]

During 1699 work continued on the large St. Ulrich (III+P/48) and St. Jakobi (III+P/37) organs in Magdeburg; contracts were negotiated for three new organs (Ganderkesee, Buxtehude, and Clausthal-Zellerfeld); and the rebuild of the old St. Ulrich organ was undertaken for St. Petri in Magdeburg. In addition, repairs were accomplished in Hamburg-Steinbeck and at St. Lamberti/Oldenburg at the same time as organs were being completed in Groningen (II/16), Kloster Berge (near Magdeburg, I+P/13), Dargum/Mecklenburg (II+P/22), St. Gertrudis in Hamburg (II+P/21), and Ganderkesee.

Conflict with Schnitger's major rival reared its head again as Joachim Kayser attempted in 1699 to secure contracts for repairs in Jade and in Westerstede, the latter his own opus. Schnitger protested, asking King Christian V to protect his privilege for Oldenburg and Delmenhorst and to "have the church officials [in the Oldenburg duchy] gravely ordered not to lend the slightest help to the 'foreign' organ builder."[15] As a result, Kayser was not even permitted to maintain the organ he had built in Westerstede. He countered with a petition to Duke Karl Wilhelm (1667–1718) in Anhalt asking for equal concessions in the Duchy of Jever and was granted the following privilege on July 21, 1699:

> Witness herewith, after the organ builder Joachim Kayser has presented most humbly that which until this time he has been able to earn here, also in East Frisia and elsewhere, with his organ building;
>
> that now some privileged people were appointed in the neighborhood, that further he was not permitted to work there and has therefore petitioned us that we would most graciously deign to give him the same concession, when it was reported to us that the suppliant, Kayser, has a good reputation in his work; and also in the organs which he has

> built in this district, he has carried out the work very well and in such a way that one was very satisfied with him;
> therefore, by virtue of these rights and privileges we have herewith conceded to him that he alone may carry out in the land we rule, namely Jever, any organ work that is necessary; we command accordingly all our [civil] servants, especially our district court here, to protect actively the above-mentioned Joachim Kayser under these rights and privileges for Jever and in no fashion to stand in his way, according to which everyone will acknowledge that we have in this document commanded that there be set forth this concession over our own signature and great seal.[16]

As a result, Kayser maintained his position in Jever and extended his activity as far as Ostfriesland and the Dutch province of Groningen (at Farsum), building new organs in St. Stephanus/Fedderwarden (1702), Wilhelmshaven-Heppens (1703), and Eilsum (1709). Regardless of the privilege, however, in 1705 Schnitger was given precedence over Kayser in Accum; and in 1710 Gerhard von Holy, noted Schnitger journeyman, received the contract for the Stadtkirche in Jever in preference to Kayser.

1700–1719

Schnitger's first wife, Gertrud, died in 1707. This blow was followed closely by the tragically early demise of his sons, Hans in 1708 and Arp in 1712. Hans, who drowned while swimming in the Elbe River, was involved in 1708 in the construction of a new organ in Hamburg-Ochsenwerder. Apparently his body was never recovered, for the Neuenfelde funeral register states that "a memorial service was held for him in the evening of August 22, 1708, in the house."[17] The plague of 1712, which claimed some 12,000 lives in Hamburg as a grim consequence of the Swedish-Danish war, was responsible for the deaths of the younger Arp Schnitger and his cousin Hinrich Huss, son of Berendt Huss.

Added to the emotional strain of these events was the physical toll exacted by Schnitger's active organ construction in widely separated locations. On February 28, 1699 the Danish king had recognized Schnitger's supremacy and granted him a monopoly for the districts of Oldenburg and Delmenhorst. It gave him the right "alone to build and repair organs in these lands and their dependencies . . . so that if a church needs an organ built or its present instrument repaired, he alone is to be employed for reasonable reward [*gegen billige Belohnung allein gebraucht*] and in no way is this right to be impaired by any other builder."[18] By virtue of this "privilege" Schnitger was able to subcontract lesser work to his journeymen.

The "purest" of the Dutch Schnitgers was completed in 1701 in Uithuizen, at the Reformed Church (II+P/28). Few alterations have been made, and the disposition today is much as Schnitger left it.

Amazingly enough, Schnitger's work was known as far as Spain and Portugal, and in 1701 he completed two small organs (II/12) for export to the latter country. It is possible that the Faro Cathedral organ incorporates one of these earlier works, but records are sketchy, and the organ is generally attributed to Johann Hinrich Ulenkampf (João Enriques Hulenkampf) in 1715–16.

Buxtehude again summoned Schnitger in 1707, but the trip to Lübeck only led to another frustration. Schnitger was so disappointed when he was denied the commission that he refused the paltry six thalers offered by the church officials as recompense for his expenses. Two years later, after reconsideration, the amount was increased by ten thalers and sent to Schnitger in Hamburg, where it was again refused. By this time, Buxtehude, discouraged and aging, wrote to Copenhagen regarding another builder. In 1704 a relatively minor repair of the Marienkirche organ was effected by Otto Dietrich of Hamburg, who also added a Vox Humana 8′, Sesquialtera 2f., and Dulzian 16′ to the Rückpositiv. These apparently proved

Hervormde Kerk, Uithuizen[19]

Hoofdwerk (Manual I)

S	1.	Praestant	8′
	2.	Bourdon	16′
S	3.	Holpijp	8′
S	4.	Octaaf	4′
S	5.	Spitsfluit	4′
S	6.	Quint	3′
	7.	Fluit	2′
S	8.	Mixtuur	4st.
	9.	Trompet	8′
S	10.	Vox humana	8′

Rugwerk (Manual II)

	1.	Praestant	4′
S	2.	Holpijp	8′
	3.	Viola da Gamba	8′
S	4.	Fluit	4′
S	5.	Octaaf	2′
S	6.	Woudfluit	2′

Rugwerk (cont.)

	7.	Flageolet	1′
S	8.	Sexquialter	2st.
	9.	Carillon	3st.
S	10.	Dulciaan	8′

Pedal

	1.	Subbass	16′
S	2.	Octaaf	8′
	3.	Bourdon	8′
S	4.	Octaaf	4′
S	5.	Nachthoorn	2′
S	6.	Bazuin	16′
S	7.	Trompet	8′
S	8.	Cornet	2′

Manual Couplers (Hinsch)
Pedal Coupler HW/P (v. Oeckelen)
Pitch: ½ tone above normal
Wind pressure: 84 mm WS

S: existing pipe work built by Schnitger[20]

unsatisfactory, and the following year Rudolf Meyer of Schnitger's workshop was engaged to overhaul the work. Since Meyer served as Schnitger's journeyman until 1713, we can be fairly certain that he received his materials from Schnitger. It is a sad commentary (and one that relates to repeated occurrences down through the years) that Buxtehude did not live to see the complete renovation of his organ.

The last decade or so of Schnitger's life was fraught with the deterioration of his finances, despite his ownership of three spacious houses in Hamburg (two near the Katharinenkirche and the harbor and one on the Pferdemarkt near St. Jacobi). The first two had passed to Schnitger in 1693 through his wife Gertrud, having been purchased in 1668 by her father,

Hans Otte. Schnitger acquired the third house in 1708 as mortgage holder in a liquidation sale by the previous owner, Hinrich von Cöllen.

The unfortunate treatment Schnitger received at the hand of King Frederick I gives valuable insight into the final years of the master's life. In 1706 Schnitger was hastily summoned by Queen Sophie Charlotte to build an organ for the chapel in the west complex of the Charlottenburg Castle in Berlin. Known in art history as the Eosander-Kapelle, the chapel was part of the addition to the castle supervised by the famous architect Eosander von Göthe in 1704–1706. The necessity for the haste was that the chapel was not to be inaugurated until the organ had been completed. Schnitger began construction of the instrument in his Hamburg workshop and then entrusted the on-site supervision to his senior journeyman, Lambert Daniel Kastens. This delegation of responsibility irritated one Johann Nette, itinerant organ builder, who had overhauled part of the Marienkirche organ in Lübeck for Buxtehude in 1686 and had built an organ for the Royal Palace-Knight's Chapel in Berlin in 1700. Feeling slighted because he was not the choice for the Eosander-Kapelle project (after having moved from Dresden to Berlin with his entire family on the assurance of the king that he would be guaranteed an annual subsistence for organ maintenance), Nette complained that "somebody by the name of Lambertus, who, as far as I know, is not equal to his task"[21] was working on the new organ in Charlottenburg. On April 22, 1706, at his own request and as an obvious gesture of pacification, Nette was appointed Court Organ Builder, with an annual stipend of 150 Rtl. and responsibility for the maintenance of the Royal Palace-Knight's Chapel organ. Several months later, in October 1706, Schnitger took over the supervision of the installation and also secured contracts for a large (III+P/40) instrument for St. Nikolai (1706–1708) and a smaller one (II+P/24) for St. Sebastian. During the course of the Charlottenburg organ construction, Schnitger was apparently promised the position of Court Organ Builder, in charge of maintaining the organs in the Cathedral, the Palace chapels of Oranienburg and Potsdam, and subsequently those at Charlottenburg and in the Royal Palace-Knight's Chapel.

The situation of the Eosander-Kapelle organ is most unusual. It is placed against the wall on the long side of the chapel, the Rückpositiv resting on the parapet of the center niche. A narrow passageway separates it from the console, Hauptwerk, Pedal, and four bellows; thus the radiation of sound from the Hauptwerk and Pedal is somewhat inhibited. Nevertheless, the 26 voices of the three divisions more than do justice to the works of the Baroque.

EOSANDER-KAPELLE, BERLIN

Hauptwerk (Manual II)		*Rückpositiv* (cont.)	
Principal	8′	Waldflöit	2′
Flöit dues	8′	Sesquialtera	2f.
Gedact	8′	Scharff	3f. (1′)
Octav	4′	*Pedal*	
Viol de gamb	4′		
Nassat	3′	Subbass	16′
Super Octav	2′	Octav	8′
Mixtur	5f. (1⅓′)	Octav	4′
Hoboy	8′	Nachthorn	2′
Vox Humana	8′	Mixtur	6f. (2′)
Rückpositiv (Manual I)		Posaunen	16′
		Trommet	8′
Principal	8′	Cornet	2′
Lieblich Gedact	8′		
Octav	4′	Tremulant	
Flöit dues	4′	Pitch: nearly a whole tone below normal	
Octav	2′		

Despite conclusive evidence in the Deutsches Zentralarchiv, there continues to be controversy over the authenticity of this organ, which admittedly varies from the typical Schnitger instrument. In a letter dated November 6, 1706, sent from

Charlottenburg to a Pastor Bremer in Jade/Oldenburg, Schnitger wrote:

> I would have liked to have visited you last summer, but was prevented, since I was requested to be in this place where I am building a precious work in her chapel in Charlottenburg for Her Royal Majesty in Prussia, a work which I hope to complete with the help of God within three or four weeks. The chapel, unique in every respect, is to be inaugurated not more than a week after the nuptuals [the wedding of the crown prince, later King Friedrich Wilhelm I, to Sophie Dorothea von Hannover on November 14, 1706]; so I have to remain until that is over, hoping by God to be in your vicinity shortly after Christmas and to see you then. . . .

Further confirmation of Schnitger's handiwork is contained in a petition written to the king in July 1708:[22]

> MOST SERENE AND MIGHTY MAJESTY, MOST GRACIOUS LORD: Your Royal Majesty will graciously remember that I built the organ in Charlottenburg within a short time and, I hope, to Your Royal Majesty's pleasure, and that I was ordered to keep in good order and under close inspection the other organs in the Royal Palace-Knight's Chapel, in the Cathedral, in Orianienburg and Potsdam; being most graciously promised a yearly salary of 400 Rtl. I have most humbly complied with this order and with my journeymen have taken care of all these works since Michaelmas 1706, but have received nothing as of now. Since, Most Gracious King and Lord, I have applied my best efforts caring for these organs and mean to continue, I implore your Royal Majesty most graciously to issue an order to the effect that my appointment as Court Organ Builder entailing an annual income of 400 Rtl. beginning Michaelmas 1706, when I took up my post, may be confirmed. Trusting that my request will most graciously be granted, unto death,
>
> Your Most Serene, all-powerful King,
> Most Gracious Royal Majesty's
> most humble servant,
> ARP SCHNITGER

Eosander endorsed this request by a simultaneous petition:[23]

> Your Royal Majesty has had conveyed to the organ builder your promise to keep him in your service because the man is indispensable and urgently needed for the care of the organs in the Palace, in the Cathedral, in Charlottenburg, Oranienburg and Potsdam. Should this man leave here, all organs would be idle, because no organ in the world can survive a year without repairs. This man being, moreover, the most capable and honest of his profession in all Germany. Further, his organs cost only half as much as others and are immeasurably better and more durable, the Charlottenburg organ being a good example! He has declared, however, that he cannot service the organs mentioned for less than 400 Rtl., a sum he can easily obtain elsewhere. Now 150 Rtl. are provided for the care of the Royal Palace organ and 50 Rtl. for the Cathedral organ, so that another 200 Rtl. has to be made available for the maintenance of the Potsdam, Charlottenburg and Oranienburg organs. This man has already supplied this service since Michaelmas 1706, and he humbly requests that his appointment may be from that day.
>
> Berlin, August 6, 1708 v. EOSANDER

Finally, Schnitger's appointment materialized, dated September 1, 1708:[24]

> His Royal Majesty of Prussia has most graciously ordered Arp Schnitger to be appointed and confirmed Court Organ Builder; thus he shall serve faithfully and obediently, endeavoring to seek and promote the king's best advantage, to do his utmost, on the other hand, to prevent, warn against, and avert damage and harm, particularly to take constant care of the organ in the Palace-Knight's Chapel here as well as those in the Cathedral and in Potsdam, Oranienburg and Charlottenburg; to keep them in good order, to replace damaged or worn-out parts without delay at his expense, and in general do and observe everything expected from a faithful and diligent organ builder. Whereas for these, his faithful services and work, His Royal Majesty

> has graciously promised and assured annually four hundred Thalers, i.e., 50 Th. from the Cathedral budget, 150 Th. from the Royal Treasury, and 200 Th. from his privy purse. Therefore, Messrs. Matthias von Berchem, von Stosch, and Treasurer Anwandter are herewith graciously ordered to make such payments to him from Crucis 1706, when he commenced his services, annually and against receipt.
>
> Cölln, September 1, 1708

Schnitger was thwarted again, however, and had to deal with an unnamed mediator who tried to persuade him to waive part of his salary because of difficulties with the Treasury. The following report was rendered in late September:

> I have spared no effort to get Arp Schnitger to content himself with 300 Th., but he could not be moved, protesting that 400 Rtl. had been offered to him in Hamburg and that the offer was still open; that he would rather accept that than be content with the 300 Th. here, especially since there he would be able to make some money beside his services, which was not possible here (he said), the religious corporations being poor and unable to have anything done. Also, here he personally had to pay for his trips to Potsdam and Oranienburg, and needed three or four journeymen all the time. I report the above without comment, leaving the decision to His Excellency.[25]

On December 4, 1708, for the privilege of the appointment, received at last through additional intervention by Eosander, Schnitger paid a fee of 100 Rtl. to the General-Charge-Cassa in Cölln-on-the-Spree. Again and again during his tenure as Prussian Court Organ Builder, he was forced to submit requests for the honorarium that was rightly his, as he did on January 30, 1712:[26]

> Since, however, Most Gracious King and Lord, of the 50 Rtl. graciously assigned to me from the Cathedral budget [according to the appointment document] I have as yet received nothing, not even a Groschen although I have re-

peatedly asked for, with respect, and requested the money which I counted on for myself and my dependents, the journeymen and apprentices I need, having relied on it. For six years I have run into debt (which can be proved), and now the creditors are clamoring for payment, threatening me with legal action, while I, a stranger here, get no advice or help and find myself in real need. Therefore, to Your Royal Majesty I direct my most humble, submissive request and plea that, since nothing can be expected from the Cathedral revenue (so it seems), you may grant to me the great royal grace of giving orders to the Receiver of General Domains and Court Paymaster, von Berchem, to pay to me on the forthcoming Reminiscere not only the 150 Rtl. plus 50 Rtl., making a total of 200 Rtl. annually, but also the balance unpaid since Crucis 1706, immediately and in order to satisfy my creditors. I trust in Your most gracious expedient consideration, remaining in deepest devotion all my life until I die, Your Royal Majesty's most humble, faithful, obedient servant,

ARP SCHNITGER, ROYAL COURT ORGAN BUILDER

On June 30, 1712 Schnitger received the following humiliating reply to this (or possibly even a later unrecorded) urgent plea: "The supplicant's request is refused and he is asked not to molest His Royal Majesty with this matter any more."[27]

When Friedrich Wilhelm I ascended to the throne and, in connection with his austere economic measures, dismissed Eosander, Schnitger lost all interest in his Berlin activity. The last trace of his work there is found in a correspondence of March 22, 1714, wherein he calls the great cathedral organ an "old, dilapidated work in need of major repair, or even better, renovation."[28]

The partially extant Insel Pellworm/Nordfriesland and Abbehausen/Oldenburg organs (both II+P/24) had their dedications in 1711 and 1713 respectively. The latter occasion coincided with Schnitger's marriage to Anna Elisabeth Diekmanns Koch on July 21, 1713. While building the Abbehausen/ Oldenburg organ between 1710 and 1713, Schnitger had been a guest in the home of Frau Koch, widow of the church's organist and sexton, Gerhard Koch, who had died in 1706. The Abbehausen partrimonial register gives some insight into the character of Schnitger's second wife:

> On the 21st day of August, A.D. 1713, Anna Elisabeth Koch, nee Diekmanns, presently the wife of Arp Schnitger, Royal Privileged and far-famed maker of organs, donated and gave to this Abbehausen church the sum of 12 Rtl.; and were such 12 Rtl. at once handed over to the present church committee so that the grave site south of the church door of her first and blessed husband Gerhard Koch, who for 24 years was a faithful organist and sexton, should be taken care of out of the interest, and never be opened.[29]

Schnitger had not been particularly well before his remarriage. In 1712, when the Council of Tangermünde asked him to inspect the organ at St. Stephani after repairs had been made by Johann Michael Röder, Schnitger lay ill in Bremen. He suggested that Vincent Lübeck be appointed in his place. From a letter Lübeck wrote to the councilmen of Zwolle, the Netherlands, on October 11, 1718, recommending that Schnitger build the new organ for the Michaelskerk, we know that Lübeck inspected some twenty Schnitger organs during his career.

The final efforts of Arp Schnitger were directed between October and December 23, 1718 toward the proposal for the organ at St. Michael's in Zwolle. However, illness and death overtook him, and he was buried at the Hamburg-Neuenfelde church on July 28, 1719. His design for the magnificent instrument (III+P/46) was slightly altered by his son, Franz Caspar, and carried through to completion in 1721. Beset by insurmountable professional disappointments in his last decade, Schnitger was moved to express himself thus toward the end of his life:

Many people may think that I earned much money with my work, and that there is some left; however, this is not so because
1. I never asked very much, but rather, when some churches did not possess sufficient means, I built organs for half price for the glory of God;
2. After I made a good name for myself with my work, I was often called great distances away, which necessitated a great deal of expense. I have rarely been reimbursed for traveling back and forth;
3. My various business activities at different places required many journeymen; and since I could only be present in one place at a time, many of the journeymen began seeking only their own advantage.
Finally, during the long period necessary for completing a work there were many expenses; therefore, what I gained on one organ, I lost on the next.[30]

St. Petri und St. Pauli, Cappel. Schnitger, 1680. 17. Prospekt. 18. Manuals with later added F♯ and G♯.

19, 20. Church of St. Stephan, Schortens. 21. Organ Prospekt. Joachim Kayser, 1686.

ANNO
1686
PETRUS
St IOHANNIS
St ANDREAS
St THOMAS
JACOB
EILERS
TADICK
GERCKE
LUBBEN
ONCKEN

Organ at St. Stephan, Schortens. *Upper left,* 22. Manuals and stops. *Upper right,* 23. Prinzipal 8' (Prospekt pipes), Gedackt 8' (some pipes closed, some open), Oktave 4', Rohrflöte 4'. *Below,* 24. Hauptwerk. Gedackt 8' (1686), Rohrflöte 4' (1936), Nasard $2\frac{2}{3}'$ (1936), Oktave 2' (1686). *Opposite:* 25. Detail of Prospekt showing date of original construction.

VERSTANSEN
PET. G. HAIEN
euch reichlich wohnen
vermahnet euch selbst
und
und
KOL 3,16.

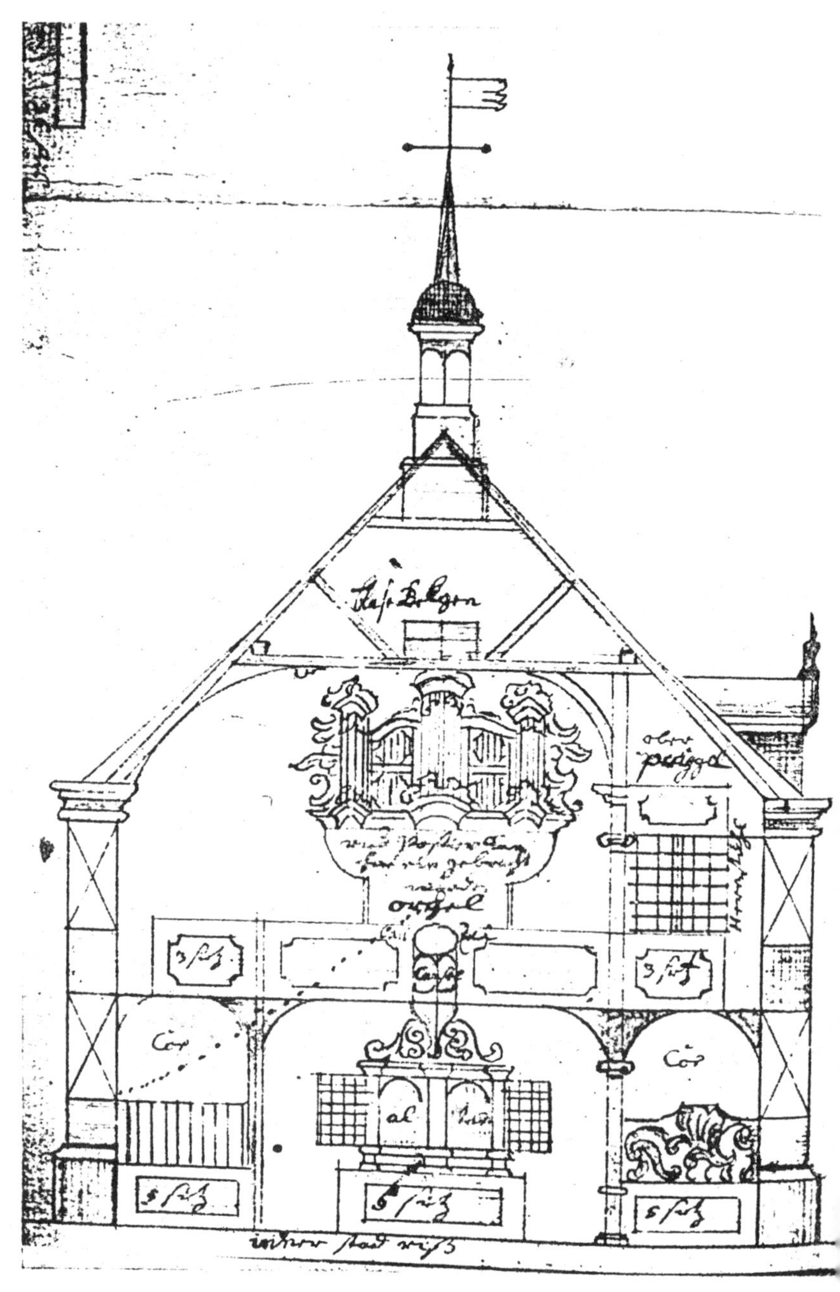

26. Schnitger's drawing for the organ at Wittmund, 1684.

27. Organ at Hohenkirchen. Joachim Kayser, 1694–95.

28. Main organ at Marienkirche, Lübeck. M. Barthold, 16th century.

29. Organ at St. Johannis, Magdeburg. Schnitger, 1689–95. Destroyed in World War II.

Organ at Hervormde Kerk, Noordbroek. Schnitger, 1695–96. 30. Manual trackers. 31. Console (manuals, Hinsch, 1768). *Opposite:* 32. Prospekt.

KNOCK
ENDE HEER
AMSINGH ENDE E
KERKVOOGDEN
IS DIT ORGEL

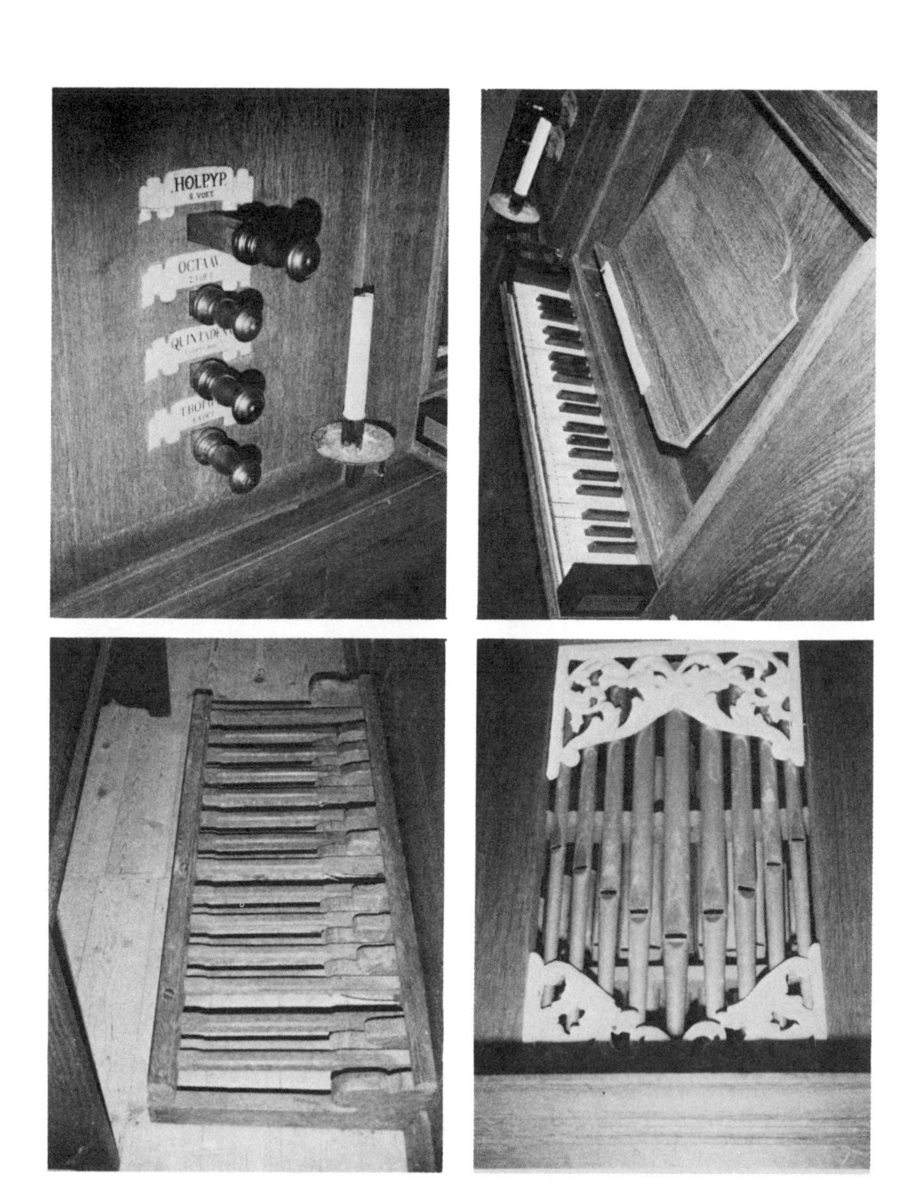

Organ at Hervormde Kerk, Nieuw Scheemda. Schnitger, 1695. 33. Stops to left of manual. 34. Manual, showing short octave C, D, E, F, G, A through c'''. 35. Pedalboard, showing short octave C, D, E, F, G, A through d'. 36. Prospekt Praestant 4'.

37. Organ at St. Bartholomäus, Golzwarden. Schnitger, 1698.

Organ at Hervormde Kerk, Pieterburen. Schnitger, 1696–98. 38. Schnitger's drawing for the organ. 39. Rugpositief facade, Allert Meijer, 1701. *Opposite:* 40. Organ as now situated in Hervormde Kerk, Mensingeweer.

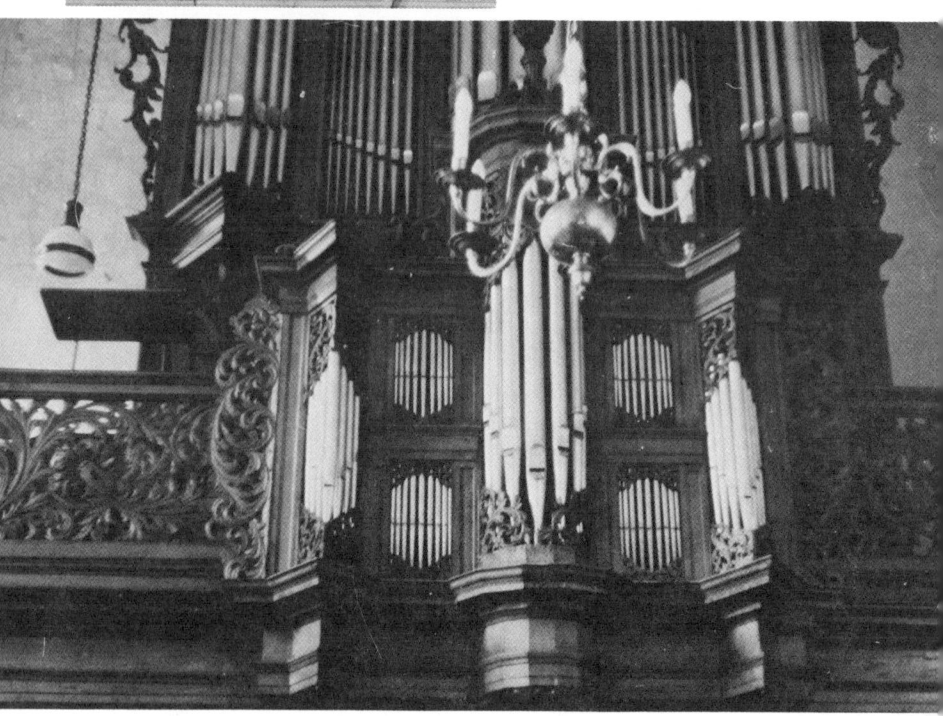

41. Christian V of Denmark, who granted Schnitger's organ-building privilege for Oldenburg and Delmenhorst, 1699.

42. Console of the Dom organ, Lübeck. Schnitger, 1696–99.

Opposite: 43. Organ at St. Willehad, Accum. Schnitger, 1705.

Organ at Hervormde Kerk, Uithuizen. Schnitger, 1700–1701. 44. Manuals. 45. Pedalboard. 46. Prospekt. 47. Dulciaan 8′, Rugwerk.

48. Sophie Charlotte, queen of Prussia.

49. Friedrich I, king of Prussia.

50. Organ at Eosander-Kapelle, Berlin. Schnitger, 1706.

Know'st thou yesterday, its aim and reason? Work'st thou well today for worthier things?
—GOETHE

3. Debt to the Past

GOETHE, the master poet might well have been asking these questions retrospectively of the master organ builder, for Arp Schnitger's retention of concepts and materials utilized by his predecessors is evident in many of his opuses. The Hamburg Jacobikirche organ, one of his most famous, boasts many ranks by Scherer and Fritzsche among the 55 registers existing from Schnitger's construction. Norden's Ludgerikirche organ was originally the output of Andreas de Mare and Edo Evers; and Schnitger's first nine projects following his apprenticeship involved the completion of contracts negotiated by his teacher, Berendt Huss, three for new organs and six for repairs. It was in Huss's 1661 creation for the Stadtkirche in Glückstadt that Schnitger found the best example of a moderate-sized organ, versatile and well balanced, the epitome of seventeenth-century ingenuity.

To this general scheme Schnitger was to add his trademark, aliquots (mutations), with their narrow scales and unique tonal qualities, perhaps the most notable of *his* "worthier things." Schnitger's respect for "the aim and reason" of yesterday explains to some extent the inconsistencies, such as scaling differences, that are present in his organs of comparable size and disposition. Divergent scalings abound, depending on the footsteps in which he might have followed and the peculiar acoustical properties with which he dealt in each construction situation. Preeminent, though, was the sharp, brilliant sound when each project was completed.

STADTKIRCHE, GLÜCKSTADT[1]

Hauptwerk		*Rück Positiv* (cont.)	
Praestante	8′	Sesquialtera	3f.
Quintadena	16′	Scharff	4f.
Rohrflöte	8′	Rankett	16′
Gedact	8′	Krumbhorn	8′
Octave	4′	*Pedahl*	
Koppelflöte	4′		
Gemshorn	2′	Octaven Bass	8′
Mixtur	6f.	*Undersatz	8′ (16′?)
Trommete	8′	*Gedact Bass	4′ (8′?)
Schalmeye	4′	Mixtur Bass	6f.
Rück Positiv		Posaunen Bass	16′
		Trommeten-Bass	8′
Praestante	4′	Cornett Bass	4
Quintadena	8′		
Gedact	8′	6 Bellows, 7′ × 4′	
Spitzflöte	4′	2 Tremulants	
Octave	2′		

*It is possible that these two stops were 16′ and 8′ respectively, both being stopped.

Stade: St. Cosmae

According to church accounts, Schnitger was active as a journeyman to Huss during the building of the organ at St. Cosmae in Stade, and he personally received payment as Huss's representative upon the completion of the instrument in 1673. St. Cosmae (dedicated to the twin brothers Cosmas and Damian, martyrs beheaded in A.D. 303 in Asia Minor) possessed an organ as early as 1493. Repairs in 1591 to a 1538 organ were attributed to Hans Scherer, the Elder; in 1606–1608, Antonius Wilde of Otterndorf added two Pedal towers and a Rückpositiv. Additional repairs were made in 1628–29 by Hans Scherer, the Younger, and in 1635 by an unknown builder from Lübeck. Extensive renovations in 1656–59 included several new voices by Hans Riege of Hamburg. Fire, that dread nemesis of so many early organs, destroyed the church and the refurbished organ in 1659; and although the church was immediately rebuilt, the contract with Berendt Huss for a new organ was delayed for ten years. During this time a Positiv purchased from Thomas Selle, a Hamburg cantor, served as substitute. Huss completed the Oberwerk, Rückpositiv, and Brustwerk between 1668 and 1671. Later, the building of the free-standing Pedal, which contained ten voices in two Pedal towers, was negotiated under a separate, special contract. In 1673 the completed instrument was approved by a Lüneburg organist, most likely Christian Flor, who served both St. Lamberti and St. Johannis there. As fate would have it, Arnoldus Schleper, the organist at St. Cosmae, lived only a matter of months following completion of the organ, and his position went to the twenty-year-old Vincent Lübeck, who quickly became esteemed as a performer, composer, teacher, and organ expert.

Lübeck was born in Padingbüttel, north of Bremerhaven. He became acquainted with Arp Schnitger at the time of his appointment to the music post at St. Cosmae. Their friendship grew during the ensuing eight years, before Schnitger moved to Hamburg. In later years they frequently encountered each other during organ inspections, complementing and furthering each other by exchanging opinions on problems of construction and design. (Interestingly enough, Lübeck later succeeded to the post of organist at St. Nikolai in Hamburg because of the inability of the previous musician to do justice to Schnitger's glorious instrument of 1687! In 1696 the old organist, Conrad Möhlman, was deemed inadequate and was replaced on occasion by a substitute, Jürgen Bronner, organist of the Holy Spirit Hospital. Complaints about Möhlman became so frequent that in 1702 he was dismissed with an annual pension of 600 M. Lübeck's appointment followed that summer, and he held the post until his death in 1740.)

In 1688 Lübeck commissioned Schnitger to make some notable changes in the disposition of the St. Cosmae organ for the sum of 400 M. They included a Trommet 16′ and Cimbel 3f. in the Oberwerk and a Krumphorn 8′ and Schalmey 4′ in the Brustwerk, changes mentioned by Schnitger in his personal records. In 1702, before Lübeck assumed the Hamburg post, Schnitger made further repairs to the organ.

Documented specifications from the tenure of the organist J. D. Wiedeburg, which began in 1732, combined with those mentioned by Niedt-Mattheson, give conclusive evidence that the renovation executed for 925 M. in 1727-28 by Otto Dietrich Richborn of Hamburg, one of Schnitger's former journeymen, changed nothing in the Huss-Schnitger scope of voices. Toward the end of the eighteenth century, accumulated dust and several minor defects necessitated an overhaul of the organ. During the course of this work, which was entrusted to Georg Wilhelm Wilhelmy of Stade at a cost of 300 Rtl., the Oberwerk Cimbel 3f. was replaced by a Rauschpfeife 2f., the Pedal Cornet 2′ by a Trompete 4′, and the four lowest metal pipes of the Subbass 16′ (C D E F) by wooden ones. According to church accounts, the organ balcony was rebuilt at that time, though the Rückpositiv retained its position. Possibly the Pedal towers were also altered through elevation, while the Principal 16′ frontal pipes were either shortened or replaced. Two arches marked with the date 1782 were built between the Pedal towers and the Oberwerk.

Church bureaucracy interfered with the next stage in the life of the organ, causing a two-year delay in negotiations following repeated pleas of the organist, Johann Wilhelm Sauerbrey, for urgently needed repairs. In 1835 Johann Georg Wilhelmy was approached for an estimate; after two years of indecision, the church officials then asked for a competitive estimate from Peter Tappe of Verden. Tappe immediately suggested replacement rather than renovations, including "a new wind-chest for the manual, because the present, so-called spring wind-chest, which may have been made four or five hundred years ago during episcopal times, can no longer serve adequately." Further suggestions included the replacement of the Nassat 1⅓′ by a Gemshorn 2′ and the Tertia 1³/₅′ by a Quinte 3′. As for the Sedetz 1′, which he wished to replace with a Fugara 4′, he remarked: "This voice does not deserve a space in the organ, for it is really too small, so that one can never hear the overtones."[2] The changes were fortunately entrusted to Wilhelmy, who finally received the commission in 1837. Sauerbrey's report reveals that the eight bellows were newly lined with leather and their valves enlarged, all wind-chests were thoroughly overhauled, the pedalboard was recessed four to six inches farther back into the case, three new manuals were installed with a new coupler between the Oberwerk and the Rückpositiv, and the Glockenspiel was made playable again. Quite a number of smaller pipes that had been damaged by martens were replaced by good pipes from another organ, and the remainder of the pipe work was removed, cleaned, and repaired. In order to make tuning easier, the lower portions of the Pedal towers were brought forward several inches so that some of the Subbass 16′ and Octav 8′ pipe work could be repositioned. Wilhelmy also altered the original tuning of the organ at this time and completed the renovation in 1841.

Thirty years later, in 1870, Johann Hinrich Röver was commissioned to do extensive work, including moving the Rückpositiv to a position inside the organ at the back on the right side, a change requested by Sauerbrey during the Wilhelmy renovation to provide adequate space for a cantor. A thorough cleaning took place, and the pitch of the entire organ was lowered a whole tone by the rearrangement of the pipes on a higher level. The original disposition of the organ suffered during the course of the Röver contract: the Nassat 1⅓′ and Sedetz 1′ in the Brustwerk were lost to a Gemshorn 8′, and the original Scharf 5f. was reduced to three ranks. The Hinterwerk (formerly the Rückpositiv) was enlarged by two new voices on a new chest—Hohlflöte 8′ and Gamba 8′. The Quintadena 8′ with the addition of a lower octave became Gedackt 16′; the Waltflöt 2′ was tuned to an Octave 2′; and in the Pedal, a Dulcian 16′ was replaced by a wooden Flötenbass 8′.

Further deterioration came about during World War I, when the tin frontal pipes affecting the Principal 16′ in the Oberwerk and Pedal were requisitioned for the war effort. Fortunately the Principal 8′, hidden inside the case, was spared. Efforts to renovate the organ were frustrated by the outbreak of World War II, but a movement by Gustav Fock, culminating in the dedication of the organ as the "Vincent Lübeck Organ" on February 9, 1940 (the 200th anniversary of Lübeck's death), encouraged the church officials to restore the organ to its original specifications.

With the Göttingen builder Paul Ott in charge and organ inspector Alfred Hoppe of Verden serving as consultant, the work was accomplished between 1948 and 1949. Wiedeburg's 1732 records were an invaluable source of information; his report revealed that numerous changes were necessary. The chests and the tracker action were completely overhauled; and by using the Querflöt 8′ of the Brustwerk, the wind pressure was set to 68 mm WS, the remaining flue pipes and the reed division being changed to adapt. After 300 years the famous double spring-chests were still preserved and functioning perfectly! Because the balcony had been considerably enlarged in 1910, the Rückpositiv, though returned to its original location, remained partially hidden. The short octave in the manuals was enlarged in 1956 by adding C♯, D♯, F♯, and G♯; and C♯ and D♯ were added to the Pedal.

The 1963–66 renovation of the church affected the organ so adversely that another overhaul was necessary, and in 1972 Jürgen Ahrend of Loga began his contribution to the Stade saga. In addition to new manuals, pedalboard (pedal length, 500 mm; width, 27 mm), and bench, Ahrend replaced several

St. Cosmae, Stade[3]

Oberwerk (Manual II)

	Principal	16′
H	Quintadena	16′
H	Oktav	8′
H	Gedackt	8′
H	Oktav	4′
H	Rohrflöt	4′
H	Nassat	3′
H	Oktav	2′
H	Mixtur	6f.
	Cimbel	3f.
S	Trommet	16′
H	Trommet	8′
	Glockenspiel	

Brustwerk (Manual III)

H	Gedackt	8′
H	Querflöt	8′
H	Flöt	4′
H	Oktav	2′
H	Tertia	1 3/5′
	Nassat Quinte	1 1/3′
	Sedetz	1′
H	Scharff	3f.
S	Krumphorn	8′
S	Schalmey	4′

Rückpositiv (Manual I)

H	Principal	8′
H	Quintadena	8′
	Rohrflöt	8′
H	Oktav	4′
H	Waltflöt	2′
	Sieflöt	1 1/3′
	Sesquialter	2f.
	Scharff	5f.
H	Dulcian	16′
H	Trechter Regal	8′

Pedal

	Principal	16′
	Sub-Bass	16′
H	Oktav	8′
H	Oktav	4′
H	Nachthorn	1′
H	Mixtur	5–6f.
H	Posaune	16′
	Dulcian	16′
H	Trommet	8′
	Cornet	2′

Manual Coupler BW/HW
Tremulant
4 Stop Valves
Pitch: about ¾ tone above normal (g' = 446 Hz)
Wind pressure: 83 mm WS

H: majority of pipe work by Huss
S: majority of pipe work by Schnitger

of Ott's voices, completely restoring the organ to its original disposition. The console is quite lovely, with lower keys of boxwood, upper ones of ebony, and manual cheeks inlaid with boxwood and ebony. The measurement of the lower keys is 98 mm front to back, with a 35 mm forward surface. Especially noteworthy are the warm Principals, 16′ in the Oberwerk and 4′ in the Pedal; the Quintadena 8′ and Sieflöt 1⅓′ in the Rückpositiv; and the Schalmey 4′ and incredibly beautiful Krumphorn 8′ in the Brustwerk.

Today the organ stands in a refurbished case of brown and gold with much of its original pipe work and chestwork intact—a monument to Huss, a treasury of information regarding Schnitger's training, and an example of perseverance for those who strive to preserve authenticity.

Neuenfelde: St. Pankratius

Under the renowned Provost Johann Henricus von Finckh (whose portrait still hangs in the church), a new St. Pankratius-Kirche was constructed in 1682–83 in Neuenfelde. A new organ of 14 voices, two manuals and built-in Pedal had been constructed in 1672–73 for the old church by the Hamburg master Hans Christoph Fritzsche, and several years later it was decided to add a free-standing Pedal division with five voices. Since the original installation had only one bellows, it was doubted whether it would suffice to supply the new pipe work, so Fritzsche was contractually held responsible for any deficiencies, real or anticipated. At his death, early in 1674, a new contract was negotiated with his widow, Christina, and his prospective son-in-law, Hans Henric Cahman. Cahman agreed to undertake Fritzsche's obligations for a reassessed fee. It is interesting to note that these proceedings were witnessed by the Hamburg cantor and composer Christoph Bernhard, who signed himself "Director Musices, as invited witness," adding, "Yet no harm involved for myself and mine."

Because of their limited size, organs such as this one by Fritzsche were usually located near the altar, against the north wall of the church, to facilitate contact between organist and minister. With such an arrangement, the organist was positioned with his back toward the wall. The Pedal was either built-in or free-standing in a single tower, like the designs of the original instruments in Altenbruch and Lüdingworth. Frequently the bellows were encased in a box built outside the church on the north side. One such bellows box is preserved as a tool shed at Mittelnkirchen. Obviously, the placement and the size of the Fritzsche organ were found unsuitable once Schnitger had reassembled it in the new Pankratius-Kirche, and on February 17, 1683, he was contracted to build a new and larger organ for 2,900 M. Though the contract has not been preserved, there is a record of Schnitger's having received at the time of signing a token of eight shillings (approximately one-half Mark).

The five years that passed before completion of the contract presented no problem, for the Fritzsche organ was quite serviceable. Fully occupied by numerous building projects in Hamburg (St. Paulikirche, Pesthofkirche, and St. Nikolai), Elmshorn, Selsingen near Stade, Altona, and the large St. Ludgeri organ in Norden, Schnitger was fortunately able to set his own pace in Neuenfelde, trusting some of the work to his journeyman Daniel (most likely Daniel Klapmeyer of the family of organ builders in Glückstadt and Oldenburg). Schnitger wisely waited until the dust had cleared from the major interior work, and with the assistance of the journeymen Claus and Jacob (probably Claus von Eitzen and Jacob Frientz) and the apprentice Hinrich (undoubtedly Hinrich Huss, son of Berendt), completed the new organ within 21 weeks in 1688. Ever respectful of "the aim and reason" of his predecessors, he outfitted the Fritzsche organ with two new bass towers and three new bellows and moved it to the Pankratiuskirche in Stade. In 1721 it was sold to Bremen-Abergen, where it was erected by Nathanael Krusewitz; and in 1868 it was replaced completely by a new Furtwängler.

The present practice of having visitors to the Neuenfelde organ contribute one Mark for the maintenance of the instrument emanated from Schnitger's own concern regarding the large number of persons who walked on the case on Sundays and holidays. At his suggestion the officials requested each visitor to make a contribution of one Heller, to be collected by the warden and kept under lock in a box on the organ.

The inevitable so-called improvements also took their toll of the Neuenfelde organ throughout the next 150 years. In 1750 the Lamstedt organ builder Jakob Albrecht removed the Trichterregal from the Rückpositiv, deeming it "of no great use," and replaced it with the Krummhorn from the Oberwerk, which was subsequently replaced by a Vox Humana 8′! The Röver family of builders from Stade (who had wreaked such havoc at St. Cosmae) created similar devastation in Neuenfelde. In 1867 Johann Hinrich Röver replaced the Rückpositiv with a new Hinterwerk of six voices, retaining the Gedackt 8′, Quintadena 8′, and Blockflöte 4′ of the eleven voices. Unbelievably, in 1886, his son Hinrich removed the Mixtur and Cornet 2′ from the Pedal, in addition to changing the temperament. Modern restoration of the organ has taken place in several stages. In 1925–26 H. H. Johann and Karl Kemper of Lübeck reconstructed the Rückpositiv, replacing the missing Schnitger pipes with some from the former Scherer organ that had been in St. Aegidienkirche in Lübeck. In 1938 Paul Ott added new mixtures, reed work, and additional bellows (the old bellows box still stands to the right rear of the organ). The Schnitger wind-chests were overhauled, and a new Vox Humana 8′ was built in 1951 by von Beckerath of Hamburg. Ott returned in 1955 to change the intonation to one-half tone above normal and to lower the wind pressure to 60 mm; and his 1980 restoration of the instrument included revitalization of the original six hand-blown bellows, which are functional as an alternative to the separate electrical winding.

St. Pankratius, Neuenfelde[4]

	Rückpositiv (Manual I)	
S	Prinzipal	4′
S	Gedackt	8′
	Quintadena	8′
S	Blockflöte	4′
O,S	Quintflöte	4′
O	Oktave	2′
O	Sifflöte	1½′
O	Sesquialtera	2f.
	Terzian	2f.
	Scharf	4–6f.
	Krummhorn	8′

	Oberwerk (Manual II)	
S	Prinzipal	8′
S	Quintadena	16′
S	Rohrflöte	8′
S	Oktave	4′
S	Spitzflöte	4′
S	Nasat	3′
S	Oktave	2′
S	Spielflöte	2′
S	Rauschpfeife	2f.

	Oberwerk (cont.)	
	Mixtur	5–6f.
	Zimbel	3f.
	Trompete	8′
	Vox Humana	8′

	Pedal	
S	Prinzipal	16′
S	Oktave	8′
S	Oktave	4′
S	Flöte	4′
	Nachthorn	2′
S	Rauschpfeife	2f.
	Mixtur	5f.
	Posaune	16′
	Trompete	8′
	Cornet	2′

Couplers: OW/RP
Tremulant
6 Bellows
Pitch: nearly ½ tone above normal
Wind Pressure: 60 mm WS

S: Schnitger pipe work
O: older pipe work supplied by Kemper in his restoration

Steinkirchen

The year 1581 marked the signing of the oldest organ building contract in preservation, an agreement between the Hamburg builder Dirk Hoyer and the officials at Steinkirchen. This parish was probably the first one in Altes Land to have an organ. It was a one-manual instrument based on 6′ pitch with a range of F–g'', a''. Hoyer was engaged to add an upper octave to the Mixtur and a new voice called Quintadena "of the loveliest and liveliest of sounds to be set and made."[5] The organ was to be enlarged to two divisions by installing a Positiv with five voices ("Hohlflöte, Siflit, a tapered Octave 2', a tinkling Cimbel and a strong Regael"); and in the Pedal were to be "a good strong Bass Tromet and Bauerfloite" (rustic flute). By 1685 the organ had deteriorated so much that, according to papers Schnitger left, he entered into a contract for the construction of a new organ on a balcony to be built at the end of the nave. The completed organ consisted of Hauptwerk, Brustwerk, and two Pedal towers as well as six voices from the Hoyer instrument. Claus von Eitzen, Schnitger's journeyman, assisted with the project; and the church records indicate that he and Schnitger were also pressed into service as godfathers for a christening on December 14, 1686.

In this instrument of 28 voices Schnitger, at the age of 39, gave the world of organ building an almost perfect jewel. Among its most interesting facets are the cylindrical Gemshorn 2' in the Hauptwerk and the Pedal Posaune 16', with its unique leather-covered lead boot, which is responsible for an enviable tone quality. The organ case and balcony railing were beautifully decorated in 1691, four years after completion of the instrument, and the railing paintings and inscription honoring Schnitger are still preserved.

Fortunately, the organ was well maintained; repairs by Schnitger in 1704 and by Johann Matthias Schrieber in 1763 are documented. Distinguishing plaster draperies outlining the organ were added in 1773, when the church was extensively renovated. In 1775 Georg Wilhelm Wilhelmy completely overhauled the organ; according to the contract in the church archives, his task was to clean the instrument thoroughly, caulk the bellows and channels, put new tin foil on the frontal pipes, install a valve in the Pedal, and substitute an Oktave 8' "for the Gedackt 8' which is an elusive voice."[6] The Cimbel Sterne (Zimbelsterns) were also reworked at this point and equipped with new, deeper-tuned bells. For the entire renovation

STEINKIRCHEN[7]

Hauptwerk (Manual I)

Prinzipal	8′	Schnitger
Quintadena	16′	C–e, Schnitger; from f, Hoyer; soldered; box beards
Rohrflöte	8′	C–E, g♯″, b″–c‴, Schnitger; F–g″, a″, Hoyer
Oktave	4′	Majority of pipes prior to Hoyer
Nasat	3′	Conical; C–g, Hoyer; g–c‴, Schnitger
Mixtur	4, 5, 6f.	Completed by Schnitger; construction by von Beckerath corresponds to the original composition.
Cimbel	3f.	von Beckerath
Oktave	2′	Prior to Hoyer
Gemshorn	2′	Cylindrical; Schnitger
Sesquialtera	2f.	Schnitger; C–H 1⅓′ + ⅘′; from c 2⅔′ + 1⅗′
Trompete	8′	Schnitger

Brustwerk (Manual II)

Gedackt	8′	C–G, oak, Schnitger; from A, oak, von Beckerath
Rohrflöte	4′	Schnitger
Quinte	3′	Conical, after Schnitger
Oktave	2′	Schnitger
Spitzflöte	2′	Schnitger
Tertian	2f.	Schnitger
Scharf	3–4f.	Schnitger
Krummhorn	8′	Low octave, Schnitger; from c, Hoyer; double conical

Pedal

Prinzipal	16′	Schnitger: C, D, E inside; from F in Prospekt
Oktave	8′	Wilhelmy, from old material
Oktave	4′	Schnitger
Nachthorn	2′	von Beckerath, according to Schnitger scalings
Rauschpfeife	2f.	Partially utilizing the remaining older pipes in conjunction with new work by von Beckerath: C: 2⅔′ + 2′
Mixtur	4–5f.	Partially utilizing the remaining older pipes in conjunction with new work by von Beckerath.

Posaune	16′	Schnitger
Trompete	8′	Schnitger
Cornet	2′	Schnitger and von Beckerath

Manual couplers, BW/HW	2 Zimbelsterns
Tremulant (reconstructed by von Beckerath)	Pitch: ¾ tone above normal
	Wind pressure: 72 mm

Wilhelmy was paid 612 M., and on May 15, 1784 he was accorded an annual maintenance contract. His son, Johann Georg Wilhelmy, inherited the maintenance agreement and serviced the organ for the final time in 1840, his labors having been limited to tuning and bellows repair for several decades prior to that.

Although the extent of the work is not known, basic repairs were carried out in 1843 by Philipp Furtwängler of Elze for the sum of 325 Rtl. Because the contract for this work is not preserved, it is difficult to ascertain which builder removed or changed those voices that are decidedly neither Hoyer's nor Schnitger's work. Johann Hinrich Röver and his son serviced the organ from 1862 to 1929; and the latter, Heinrich, in his customary fashion, removed Schnitger's wooden Gedackt 8′, except for the five largest pipes, and installed a metal Gedackt 8′. In 1893 he replaced the six Schnitger wedge bellows with a compact blowing mechanism that supplied the organ with 30 degrees of wind pressure.

The organ's present condition was achieved in 1947–48 through a renovation by Rudolf von Beckerath of Hamburg, and the case was restored in 1955. The Schnitger manuals as well as the original pedalboard are preserved in the storage area behind the case work.

Norden: St. Ludgeri

The first mention of an organist at St. Ludgeri in Norden was made toward the close of the sixteenth century, in connection with a positiv organ that was sold in 1566 to make space for a new organ by Andreas de Mare of Emden. Completed shortly before Christmas 1567, de Mare's organ suffered heavily under invasions during the Thirty Years' War, and a commission for replacement was awarded on May 16, 1616 to Edo Evers of Jever. This organ, of which ten voices remain in the later Schnitger installation, had a nine-voice Hauptwerk with built-in Pedal, a three-voice Brustwerk, and a six-voice Rückpositiv. The manual compass was F G A B–g'', a'', and the Pedal began at C. Repairs, which were financed by a collection conducted in Norden and subsequently in the surrounding rural district, were made in 1648 by Jodocus Sieburg, in 1653 and 1656–57 by Lukas Königsmark, and in 1664 by Johannes Pauly.

Conversations regarding repairs and enlargement of the Evers organ gained momentum when Harringius Redolph Koch bequeathed 200 Rtl. to be used specifically for such purposes. This fact is noted in a commemorative plaque on the organ, as is the legacy of 2,000 guilders from Ulrich Hinrichs, a baker. When Koch died in 1680, efforts to increase the organ fund accelerated; and when the church accounts showed a surplus on August 2, 1681, it was decided that this money should either be invested or be used toward organ repair. From August through December 1685 there was intense competition among organ builders and their journeymen from far and wide for the execution of the work at St. Ludgeri; and on February 26, 1686 a contract was concluded with Arp Schnitger for a new construction rather than for a renovation. The contract, now lost, but available to Cremer in 1926, read:[8]

> It is herewith made known to all, particularly to those directly concerned, that on the date given below, a perma-

nent and irrevocable contract was made and concluded between, on one side, the church wardens, acting for the magistrate, ministries and the entire parish of the town of Norden, and on the other side, Arp Schnitger, organ builder from Hamburg, with the following contents, and thus:

The organ builder promises to deliver to the church in Norden a new, good and faultless organ according to his proposal dated February 26, 1686, co-signed by the cantor Hinrich Bernhard Stolzenberg [of] Norden and organist Hermanno Schmit [of] Aurich. He has proposed to use ten voices from the old organ which can be rendered usable.

In the Oberwerk:	Quintadena	16′
	Gedackt	8′
	Spitzfloit	4′
	Octave	4′
	Quinta	3′
	Super Octave	2′
In the Rückpositiv:	Quintadena	8′
	Sesquialtera	2f.
	Octave	2′
In the Pedal:	Posaunen Bass	16′

Since, however, in each of these voices C, D, E, and g, b, h and c''' are missing, and in the Pedal D, F, G, the largest of which are considerably heavy, and moreover, since the existing pipes are defective and would normally be disposed of, they will have to be reworked in order to be usable.

In the Oberwerk:	Principal	8′	
	Nasat	3′	
	Gemshorn	2′	
	Mixtur	8f.	
	Cimbel	3f.	
	Trommete	8′	
In the Rückpositiv:	Principal	8′	[low G ex-
	Octave	4′	posed, C D E F
	Waldfloit	2′	enclosed]

	Ziffloit	1′	
	Tertian	2f.	
	Scharf	6f.	
	Dulcian	8′	
In the Pedal:	Principal	16′	[low F exposed,
	Gedackt	8′	C D D♯ E
	Octave	4′	enclosed]
	Mixtur	8f.	
	Trommet	8′	
	Cornet	2′	

Altogether 29 voices.

Further, three new structures have to be made with delicate carvings, one for the Oberwerk, one for the Rückpositiv, the third for the Pedal, in accordance with the submitted drawing.

Two new manuals of beautiful lettern wood and ivory semitones, from C–c''', a total of 45 keys.

A new pedal, from C, D, D♯, E, F, F♯, G, G♯, etc. up to d', with 26 keys.

Three new wind-chests of pure seasoned wood. A new bellows, the other four newly lined so that they may pass as new.

New ducts and channels throughout the entire work, new stop and tracker action.

A new coupling so that both manuals may be coupled and the Pedal with the Rückpositiv; a valve for each chest; further a tremulant, two revolving Zimbelsterns, and all attachments, as well as springs for all chests, made of brass wire. It is expressly agreed that the old pipes which can no longer be used (except those which are used to improve the remaining pipes) shall be deducted, the remaining ones to be taken over by the organ builder for cash by weight, while anything else of the old structure and wind-chests shall be left for the use of the church.

This work now the organ builder promises to carry out with good materials to his discretion, faithfully and honestly, and to begin work immediately so as to deliver it, with the help of God, to the church of Norden at Easter next year, further to hurry the work industriously so that the complete work may be examined around June 1687 by good, capable and impartial organists and thus be found satisfactory overall, so that the old voices shall not lag behind the new ones in resonance, and the work for its agreed price shall be praised; otherwise he will be satisfied to accept, on the last-named date, a lower sum should the work be appraised for less.

For the work specified above, the churchwardens, in the name of the magistrate, ministries, and the whole parish of the town of Norden, promise to pay to the organ builder, Arp Schnitger, the sum of 1200 Rtl., in words one thousand and two hundred Reichstaler, in East Frisian or other valid currency in three installments, namely 200 Rtl. now on signing; 600 Rtl. on delivery; and 400 Rtl. one year and a day after delivery, during which time the organ builder binds himself to examine [the organ] personally, or in the case of death to have [it] examined by another qualified person appointed by his heirs, and to correct any defects which may have occurred contrary to expectations.

The church will supply the base on which the organ is to rest, further, panels, bellows case and encasement of the organ, and during the time of installation and tuning will furnish a minimum of food as well as accommodations; and the instrument shall be shipped here at the expense of the church, while the organ builder pays for FOB Hamburg.

As security that everything mentioned shall be observed honorably and honestly on both sides, the contract partners pledge the church's property and the organ builder's estates respectively, and have signed this contract by hand, confirmed by the seal of this town.

Given Norden, 26th day of February A.D. 1686.
WILHELM HARMENS SCHOTTO, Churchwarden
OIKE BOHLEN, Churchwarden
HINRICH EGGERICHS, Churchwarden

That the churchwardens of the town of Norden have today paid to me the aforementioned 200 Rtl. as the first installment stated in the contract, such is herewith acknowledged.
Norden, 26 February A.D. 1686.

ARP SCHNITGER
Organ Builder, mppria

The circumstances surrounding the 1686 contract between Schnitger and the Norden church officials represent one of those rare instances in which a congregation grows more sympathetic with the progress of an instrument. In this case a considerable enlargement of the original concept resulted. Schnitger proposed a main division with twelve voices, a Rückpositiv with ten, and a Pedal with seven—a total of 29, which included the ten voices from Evers's organ. Fortunately, the drawings for these three divisions have been preserved in the church archives, and if they were not made by Schnitger, they were at least executed in his workshop. The enlargements approved by the congregation included an Oberwerk of eight voices, a Brustwerk of six, one additional voice in the Rückpositiv, and two more in the Pedal, so that the final design consisted of 46 sounding voices, with the Oberwerk and Brustwerk sharing one manual.

As in Lüdingworth and Altenbruch, Schnitger reverted to the Old North German practice of using one Pedal tower, as it was necessary to erect the organ on a balcony to the right side of the Choir, midway of the church. The sound of the organ is amazingly well integrated because of Schnitger's decision to position the Hauptwerk and Rückpositiv at an angle to the main aisle of the church; and the Pedal division is surprisingly audible in any location. This organ boasts an especially lovely Rohrflöte 8′ by Evers and a gorgeous Waldflöte 2′ by Schnitger, in addition to the latter's notable Sesquialtera 2f. and Terzian 2f. in the Rückpositiv, and the oak Blockflöte 4′, Quinte 1½′, and Scharf 4f. in the Brustwerk. Another testament to his craftsmanship is the presence today of Schnitger chests in all divisions.

By studying the accounts of the construction of the Norden organ it is possible not only to establish a month-to-month schedule of the building procedure but also to appreciate the human element, so often overlooked in chronicles of this type. We note that at the same time Schnitger was paid his first installment, a Latin cantor, Hinrich Bernhard Stolzenberg, and an organist named Schmit, from Aurich, were reimbursed 3 guilders and 12 guilders respectively for their efforts in the negotiations of the contract. Only an insignificant part was played by Henricus Alcken, organist of St. Ludgeri since 1657, partly because of his advanced age. Even before the dedication of the organ in mid-January 1688, efforts had been made to secure a new, more-efficient organist.

As considerable funds were necessary to purchase essential materials, the income derived from the sale of an old church bell was added to the legacy of Ulrich Hinrichs. Schnitger procured the wood for the base and substructure in Hamburg for 187 guilders, but evidently allowed an undue amount of time to elapse before actively proceeding with the construction, as a lengthy correspondence between Norden and Hamburg took place during the remainder of 1686 and part of 1687. Admittedly, he was under considerable pressure at this time, with organs also in progress at Steinkirchen and at Neuenfelde, the tragedy of his infant daughter's death in 1685, and the birth of Arp in 1686 and of Hans in 1688. In May and June 1687 the dock workers and teamsters of Norden were fully occupied with unloading organ parts on the Siel; and Schnitger and several journeymen arrived in late June to find accommodations with the church's sexton, Lammert Helmich, who occupied that post for 30 years. The substructure was completed on June 16, and was celebrated by a mammoth beer party.

Throughout the installation of the various components of the organ, the local artisans and tradespeople found numerous opportunities for participation. Paul Wiemers, crate maker, supplied the oak used by Gerdt Ziammen and Tobias Dircks to turn 70 studs used in building the organ balcony. Dircks was also responsible for the 64 stop knobs. Three guilders, five schaf was paid to Johannes Deniger for the two chandeliers, and all necessary paper was supplied by the bookbinder,

Scipio Mennen. Among the items imported from Hamburg were the wood carvings beneath the organ and the paintings on the case.

As frequently occurs in this area of craftsmanship, the scheduled delivery date in June 1687 had long passed when a 30-day testing period occurred in November. For "blowing the wind" for this trial, Tiel Warnes received 12 guilders in addition to his annual stipend of 18 guilders for this occupation. Dedication of the organ was celebrated on January 25, 1688, following inspection by Hermannus Schmit. His opinion, cited on p. 118, was acknowledged by a gift of 23 guilders, 4 schaf; and such was the satisfaction of the congregation that each of the journeymen received 32 guilders, 4 schaf.

In view of the funds available, the payment of the numerous locals as work progressed, and the additions made to the original contract, it is no wonder that the treasury was exhausted before the organ was completed. The parish borrowed 500 guilders at 5 percent interest from Gerdt Taden in November 1688, but in succeeding years it found that the debt could not be repaid from surpluses in operating funds. Thus, in 1692 the "Mayor and Council, Ministry, Elders and the Most Distinguished of the Parish unanimously agreed" to conduct a solicitation of funds in the parish in order to settle the debts. Consisting of small contributions ranging from 3 schaf to 3 Rtl., the collection netted about 600 guilders. Because of this widespread involvement, the congregation was especially conscientious regarding the maintenance of the organ and continuously consulted with Schnitger about its upkeep. In 1706 he personally cleaned the organ in conjunction with the renovation of the church, the funds again being procured through a parish solicitation. Johann Diedrich Druckenmüller, the extremely capable and knowledgeable organist secured in May 1688, was largely responsible for the informed attitude of the congregation, having left to his successor (his brother, Johann Jakob) specific instructions for the preservation of the organ:

1. Since this work is full of various beautiful voices, a good organist is required who knows how to display strength, force and beauty in numerous ways through well-acquired art, so that it may be obvious that he likes good compositions and handles them well.

2. Further, he may be expected to know and understand how to tune and maintain the long- and short-resonator reeds [Rohrwerke and Schnarrwerke]. Since these suffer much from the weather, they should be tuned at least once a week if he wants to play well and purely. If they warp or are covered by nitrous film, clean diligently; otherwise the church will have great expenses and even the good name of the organ will not suffice.

3. The organist should be able to solder, so that if a resonator breaks off he is in a position to repair and solder . . . something not everyone can do because it is normally the organ builder's job.

4. The organist of this work has also to watch carefully that the bellows are well blown, so that the work does not go out of tune, particularly the mixtures, which can easily be changed by a sudden rush of wind. Also, the organist must be able to use the tuning fork lest the church have great expenses and the work eventually perish.

5. It is further fair to expect the organist to concern himself about cleanliness so that keyboards and organ are industriously cleaned by the wind blowers. Also endeavor tirelessly to keep stops and keys neat to avoid noisiness. Furthermore, if, for instance, a spring in the chests is too weak, strengthen it; and make an effort to remedy all defects.

6. One or two more things could be mentioned: however, since all things do not present themselves in the same manner, have no doubt that this work shall by God's mercy achieve, by art not luck, what shall attain to the glory of God and your own well-being.

7. It is of particular importance that the instrument be assiduously tuned on Saturdays, for that is the organist's responsibility, since there are ten Schnarrwerke within; else the organ will soon be in a state of disrepair.[9]

The tonal quality of the organ was judiciously preserved throughout large and small repairs until 1882, when efforts were directed toward adapting the instrument to then-prevailing tastes. Alteration of the original specifications occurred at the hands of the local builders, Lorentz, Diepenbrock, and Bruns; and when the frontal tin pipes were removed in 1917 for war purposes, it was discovered that only 23 of Schnitger's 46 voices remained. Restoration of the original specification was undertaken in 1929–31, under the supervision of Furtwängler and Hammer of Hannover, on the basis of a design that had been in the Norden church archives in the first half of the eighteenth century, which presumably corresponded with Schnitger's conception. The newly adopted principles of the Orgelbewegung (1925–27) greatly influenced this project, but the intended goals were not totally realized. In 1943 the organ was dismantled and stored to protect it from the ravages of World War II. An extensive renovation was begun by Paul Ott of Göttingen in 1956. Mechanical action was installed, replacing the pneumatic wind system built in 1931, and a new console was added. A thorough historical restoration by Jürgen Ahrend is scheduled for the near future.

St. Ludgeri, Norden[10]

Hauptwerk (Manual II)

Prinzipal	8′	In Prospekt, F. and H., zinc
Quintadena	16′	Prior to Schnitger; C, D, E, Schnitger
Rohrflöte	8′	Edo Evers; from d'', F. and H.
Oktave	4′	Prior to Schnitger (de Mare or Evers)
Spitzflöte	4′	F. and H.
Quinte	3′	F. and H.
Nasat	3′	F. and H.
Oktave	2′	Prior to Schnitger
Gemshorn	2′	Cylindrical, Schnitger
Mixtur	8f.	F. and H. and Ott
Zimbel	3f.	F. and H.
Trompete	16′	F. and H.

Rückpositiv (Manual I)

Prinzipal	8′	In Prospekt, F. and H., zinc
Gedackt	8′	Prior to Schnitger

Oktave	4′	Schnitger
Rohrflöte	4′	Schnitger and Ott
Oktave	2′	Prior to Schnitger
Waldflöte	2′	Cylindrical, Schnitger
Sifflöte	1′	Schnitger
Sesquialtera	2f.	Prior to Schnitger; C, D, E, Schnitger; C: 1⅓′ + ⅘′; from c': 2⅔′ + 1⅗′
Terzian	2f.	Schnitger, C: ⅘′ + ⅔′; c°: 1⅗′ + 1⅓′; from c': 3⅕′ + 2⅔′
Scharf	6f.	F. and H.
Dulzian	8′	F. and H.

Oberwerk (Manual III)

Holzflöte	8′	Schnitger, C–H covered; c–h'' open conical, oak
Oktave	4′	Schnitger
Flachflöte	2′	Schnitger
Rauschflöte	2f.	F. and H.
Scharf	4–6f.	F. and H.
Trompete	8′	F. and H.
Vox Humana	8′	F. and H.
Schalmei	4′	F. and H., from c'' labial

Brustwerk (Manual IV)

Gedackt	8′	Schnitger, oak
Blockflöte	4′	Schnitger, oak
Prinzipal	2′	F. and H.
Quinte	1½′	Schnitger
Scharf	4f.	Schnitger
Regal	8′	F. and H.

Pedal

Prinzipal	16′	In Prospekt, F. and H., zinc
Oktave	8′	Possibly Schnitger
Oktave	4′	F. and H.
Rauschpfeife	2f.	F. and H.
Mixtur	8f.	F. and H.
Posaune	16′	F. and H.
Trompete	8′	F. and H.
Trompete	4′	F. and H.
Cornet	2′	F. and H.

Manual couplers, RP/HW, BW/HW, BW/OW
Pedal coupler, RP/P
Tremulants
Zimbelstern

Pitch: about ½ tone above normal
Wind pressure—Manuals: 56 mm
Pedal: 60 mm

F. and H.: Furtwängler and Hammer

51. Organ at St. Cosmae, Stade. Berendt Huss and Schnitger, 1673.

St. Cosmae, Stade. *Opposite:* 52. Console. 53. Brustwerk (front to back): Schalmey 4′ (Schnitger), Krumphorn 8′ (Schnitger), Flöt 4′ (Huss), Gedackt 8′ (Huss), Querflöt 8′ (Huss). *Above:* 54. Spring-chest. 55. Church steeple.

56. Vincent Lübeck, composer and organist at St. Cosmae. Pastel drawing c. 1710. Now in Altonaer Museum, Hamburg.

Organ at St. Pankratius, Neuenfelde. Schnitger, 1682–88, 1698. 57. Manuals and stops. 58. Bellows box.

59. Hof des Orgelbauers, the Schnitgers' home in Neuenfelde.

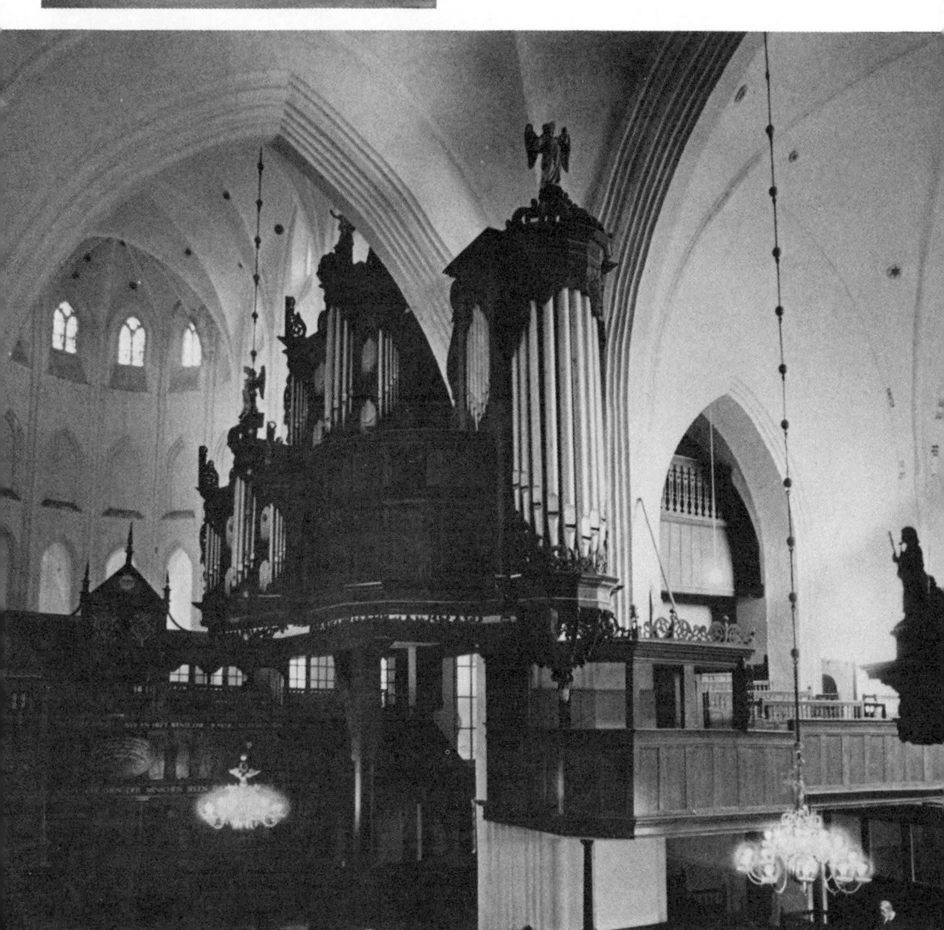

60. Organ at St. Ludgeri, Norden. Schnitger, 1687.

Organ at Steinkirchen. Schnitger, 1687. 61. Prospekt. *Opposite:* 62. Reconstructed Tremulant, Rudolf von Beckerath, 1947–48. 63. Lead wind conduits. 64. Zimbelstern.

The whole cycle impenitently revolves,
and all the past is future.
—ROBINSON JEFFERS

4. Legacy for the Future

AS important as his respect for the past is the impact of Schnitger's own work on the future. His influence is becoming more and more obvious as twentieth-century builders return to Baroque concepts of organ design. This trend is evident in the crafting of instruments primarily for the support of congregational participation such as those Schnitger built in the following communities:

Schwei/Oldenburg (St. Secundus), 1683–85 (II/14)
Middelstum/The Netherlands (Hervormde Kerk), 1695 (II/15)
Oldenbrok/Oldenburg (St. Maria; St. Nikolaus), 1696–97 (II/12)
Dedesdorf/Oldenburg (St. Laurentius), 1697 (II/12)
Strückhausen/Oldenburg (St. Johannes), 1697 (II/12)
Groningen/The Netherlands (Lutherse Kerk), 1699 (II/16)
Ganderkesee/Oldenburg (St. Cornelius und Cyprianus), 1699 (II/16)
Hamburg/Eppendorf (St. Johannis), 1700 (II/11)
Sandesneben/Lauenburg, 1701–1702 (II/15)
Esenshamm/Oldenburg (St. Matthäus), 1704–1705 (II/16)
Rastede/Oldenburg (St. Ulrich), 1709 (II/12)
Leer/Ostfriesland (Lutherkirche), 1714 (II/18)

These smaller organs have some common characteristics. In several instances, a double wind-chest accommodated both divisions. Also to conserve space, the Prinzipal 8′ was frequently eliminated and a Prinzipal 4′ in the Prospekt became the foundation of the instrument. Except for this Prospekt rank, which was usually of pure tin, the tin/lead ratio was maintained at 30 pounds of tin to 100 pounds of lead, hence the resultant tonal warmth of these organs. This aspect of their beauty has been overlooked in many descriptions of Schnitger's organs; however, it is an important consideration for the future. The magical balance between the timbres of Schnitger's mixtures and foundation stops is an especially crucial consideration in smaller organs, where every voice is exposed to its fullest extent. A fourth common component is the frequent dividing of both the Trompet and the Mixtur stops to permit greater latitude in registration. Suspension of the Pedal and the use of manual-to-pedal coupling is a feature common to all these organs, though in a number a modest independent Pedal division was added later.

Dedesdorf: St. Laurentius

The accounts of St. Laurentius in Dedesdorf include a copy of a typical Schnitger contract incorporating these design concepts.[1]

> Herewith it shall be known that on the day given below a binding contract was made between the pastors and jurats of the church of Dedesdorf on one side and Arp Schnitger, organ builder, on the other, the named organ builder taking it upon himself to construct, in the church mentioned, a new organ with the following voices:
>
> *On Upper Manual*
>
> | | | |
> |---|---|---|
> | Principal | 4′ | with 65 pipes of pure tin, highly polished |
> | Gedact | 8′ | with 47 pipes |
> | Floite | 2′ | with 47 pipes |
> | Quinta | 1½′ | with 47 pipes |
>
> *On Lower Manual*
>
> | | | |
> |---|---|---|
> | Quintaden | 8′ | with 47 pipes |
> | Gedact | 4′ | with 47 pipes |

Copia No. 2

43

Zu Wissen sey hiermit, daß am Untergesetzten dato zwischen denen (: Titt:) HH. Pastoren und Juraten der Kirchen zu Dedesdorff an einen, und [illegible] Orgelmacher am andern Theil ein beständiger Contract ist geschlossen und vollenzogen worden, es übernimbt ernandter Orgelmacher über sich in gedachter Kirchen eine Neue Orgel zu verfertigen mit folgende Stimmen, alß

Im Ober-Clavier

1. Principal ---- 4 fuß mit 65 pfeiffen von [illegible] zum wolaußgefallen,
2. Gedact ---- 8 fuß --- 47 pfeiffen;
3. flöite ---- 2 fuß --- 47 pfeiffen;
4. Quinta ---- 1½ fuß -- 47 pfeiffen;

Im Unter-Clavier

5. Quintaden ---- 8 fuß mit -47 pfeiffen;
6. Gedact ---- 4 fuß --- 47 pfeiffen;
7. Quinta ---- 3 fuß --- 47 pfeiffen;
8. Octav ---- 2 fuß --- 47 pfeiffen;
9. Sexquialt ---- 2 fach --- 94 pfeiffen;
10. Sieflit ---- 1½ fuß --- 47 pfeiffen;
11. Mixtur ---- 4 fach -- 188 pfeiffen;
12. Trommet ---- 8 fuß --- 47 pfeiffen;

Summa 12 Stimmen, darzu eine gedoppelte Windlade, da obgedachte Stimmen auff zustehen kommen, von den besten Wagenschoß, ein Tremulant, zwey gute Clavier mit [illegible] in allen 47 Clavier, ein Pedal welches an unter-Clavier gekoppelt wird, ferner werden die Clavieren gemacht daß man sie beyde zugleich, auch

Daß

65. Contract for the organ at St. Laurentius, Dedesdorf.

daß daß Pedal durch beyde Clavirn zu gebrauchen sey. Die Trommet 8 fuß und Mixtur müßen hal-
ben mit zwey Zügen gemacht werden, daß man d.
Trommet im Pedal und Mixtur zur Scharff
gebrauchen kan, Ferner drey gute Balgen
7 fuß lang 4 fuß breit, mit ihren Canalen von gu-
ten trocken Eichen holtz, die Angehenge und Federn
alle von Messing drath, alle inwendige Pfeiffen w
von Metal gemacht da auff 100 ℔ bley 30 ℔ zinn
versetzet werden soll, hierzu verschaffet der Orgelmacher
die Structur mit den Zierahten nach beygefunden Ab-
auch ferner alle Materialen wie sie nahmen hab
und machet die Arbeit gut und untadelich, daß bey der
Lieferung nichtes daran zu tadeln, so soll auch solche
Arbeit gleich angefangen und dero gestalt beschleuniget
werden daß es mit Gottes hülffe gegen Ostern 1698
kan fertig in vorgedachter Kirchen geliefert werden.

Dahingegen geloben und versprechen obbe-
nandte Contrahenten dem Orgelmacher, für solche Orgel fertig zu liefern drey hundert zwantzig Rth.
auff zwey Terminen zu bezahlen, als nach Unterschrift
des Contracts 120 rth. wan daß werck geliefert und
gut befunden, den rest als 200 rth. Lassen daß werck
auff der Kirchen Kosten aus Bremen holen und ver-
schaffen dem Orgelmacher bey auffsetzung und Stimmung
frey Logiment, nebenst nottürfftig Essen und trincken
und haben weiter mit nichts zu schaffen, Solches alles
Ehrlich zu halten, Ist dieser Contract im Nahmen
Gottes geschlossen, in duplo verfertiget, und von beyder-
seits Contrahenten unterschrieben worden, Geschen
Dedesdorff d: 16 Augusti Anno 1697.

Petrus Dreas
Pastor.
Tebbe Heinß Kirchgeschworner.
Ahlff Ehlers Kirchgeschworner.
Carsten Sanders Kirchgeschworner.

Arp Schnitger
Orgelmacher mp:

Quinta	3′	with 47 pipes
Octav	2′	with 47 pipes
Sesquialt	2f.	with 94 pipes
Sieflit	1½′	with 47 pipes
Mixtur	4f.	with 188 pipes
Trommet	8′	with 47 pipes

In all, twelve voices; further, a double wind-chest of the best heartwood where the above voices will stand; a tremulant; two good manuals with F♯ and G♯, 47 keys altogether; and a Pedal coupled with the lower manual. The manuals shall be made so they can be played simultaneously and so the Pedal can be worked by either manual. Trompet and Mixtur shall be split and made with two stops so the Trompet may be used in the Pedal and the Scharf may be separated from the Mixtur. Further, three good bellows, 7 feet long and 4 feet wide, with channels of well-seasoned oak, connections and springs all made of brass wire, and all enclosed pipes made of metal consisting of 30 lb. tin per 100 lb. lead.

For this the organ builder will supply the structure with ornaments as per the drawing attached. Further, all materials shall be supplied—and he shall do the work well and without reproach so that on delivery nothing shall be found faulty. Such work shall be begun at once and so hastened that, with the help of God, it may be completed and delivered to the above church around Easter 1698.

Whereas the named honorable opposite contract parties promise and vow to pay to the organ builder 320 Rtl. for same organ, to be paid on two occasions, i.e., 120 Rtl. after signing the contract and 200 Rtl. on delivery of the instrument, if found satisfactory. They will have the instrument brought from Bremen at the church's expense, and will furnish to the organ builder during the time of installation and tuning free accommodations and necessary sustenance. They are responsible for nothing else.

To insure the legality of all this, the contract is drawn up in the name of God, made out in duplicate, and signed by both parties. Given at Dedesdorf, 16 August Anno 1697.

Petrus Dreas, Pastor
Arp Schnitger, Organ Builder mpp.

Pastor Dreas housed Schnitger and the journeymen in his home during the 1698 summer installation, obviously enjoying their presence. When the consistory questioned the amount of beer and brandy consumed during the period of the installation, Pastor Dreas retorted: "The organ builder is a reputable man and his journeymen are nice, neat people to whom one could not offer bad beer. . . ."[2] The congregation heard the organ for the first time on July 3, 1698, following approval by the Oldenburg organist Wichardt.

Eilert Köhler, also of Oldenburg, was engaged in 1742 to disassemble the organ, repair it, and replace worn parts. This repair resulted in minor alterations to the lower manual specifications: Schnitger's Quinta 1⅓′ was replaced by a Gemshorn 2′, and the Quintadena 8′ was tuned differently. Also, a free-standing Pedal with the following stops "of good, irreproachable metal" was added:

Octave	8′	Posaune	16′
Octave	4′	Trompete	8′
Mixtur	4f.	Trompete	4′

The instrument, tuned according to the new temperament, was approved by Christoph Lanan of Oldenburg on October 29, 1745. Minor repairs were made in 1775 and 1789 by Johann Hinrich Klapmeyer of Oldenburg. The only apparent alteration until 1803 consisted of the exchanging of the Floit 2′ and the Octave 2′, noted by the organ builder Krämershoff of Oldenburg in an inspection report before he undertook repairs in 1805–1806. Typical of the period, the report read in part:

> This organ, which is completely out of tune, is in need of improvement. The reeds [*Schnarrstimmen*] are of little use, namely the three Trompeten and the Posaune. The mouths have been made unsuitably wide and are slow to respond. The wind-chests are made much too short, so the pipes cannot stand upright, as crowded as those in Esensham. . . .

> Otherwise, the instrument is not badly made. . . . The four bellows, far away from the organ on the floor of the church, supply only a weak wind; they do not open wide enough, should open half again as wide. . . . [3]

Despite the number of criticisms by Krämershoff, his repairs did not change the compass of voices. That was left to J. G. Schmid of Oldenburg, who replaced the Pedal Mixtur with a Subbass 16′ in 1838. In 1860 J. C. Schmid, also of Oldenburg, installed four new bellows; and in 1934 Furtwängler and Hammer of Hannover overhauled the organ. The frontal pipes, which vanished during World War I, were replaced by a new, 60 percent tin Praestant 4′ when Alfred Führer of Wilhelmshaven made repairs in 1957. The Führer restoration in 1978 included reconstruction of the original mechanical action components. The original keyboards remain, with ivory-lined sharps and ebony-lined naturals fitted with boxwood pegs. The front edges of the naturals are an excellent example of artistic routing. Occupying one of the most limited spaces in which Schnitger placed an organ, this instrument testifies to his design skills.

Strückhausen: St. Johannes

In 1672 Pastor Philipp Ebeling donated a positiv organ to his parish in Altenkirchen (now Strückhausen). The builder Elias (Huss?) moved the instrument to a new gallery in the St. Johannes Kirche. With the growing musical demands of the congregation, the organ became inadequate; and on August 6, 1697 a contract was signed with Arp Schnitger for a new instrument:[4]

> Be it hereby known, that on the date given below, a binding contract of the following specifications has been drawn up and executed between the Most Reverend Pastors, Magistrates and the Elders of the parish of Alten-

kirchen on the one part and Arp Schnitger, organ builder, on the other part.

The organ builder, Arp Schnitger, promises to build a new organ in the old church in which there shall be the following stops:

Upper Manual

Principal	4′	Pure English tin, well polished
Gedact	8′	
Quinta	3′	
Octav	2′	

Lower Manual

Holzfloit	8′	
Blockfloit	4′	
Nassat	3′	
Waltfloit	2′	
Sexquialt	2f.	
Mixtur	4f.	(divided)
Dulcian	16′	
Tromet	8′	(divided)

A Tremulant

In addition, two manuals with F♯ and G♯, and also a Pedal suspended from the lower manual, the two manuals provided with a coupler, so that one can use the Pedal with either manual; thereto, double wind-chests on which the above-mentioned stops are to be placed, next to them 3 bellows 7 feet long, 4 feet wide, all made from the best heartwood and oak.

Receipt

That the Most Reverend Magistrates of Altenkirchen have duly paid 50 Reichsthaler on the first date named in this contract, in witness whereof and legal receipt given.
Executed at Altenkirchen, the 6th August 1697

Arp Schnitger
Organ Builder

The old positiv organ and 324 Rtl. were Schnitger's payment for the organ, which was dedicated during the week of July 1, 1698, after having been proven by the Bremen Cathedral organist, Johann Scheele.

Flooding was an ever-present danger in Germany's northern coastal region, hence the numerous Romanesque edifices set high on wharves with windows at gallery level—reminders of a time when families, livestock included, flocked to their parish church to wait out the devastating waters. At the time of the great Christmas flood in 1717, the Altenkirchen organ suffered extensive damage, which was first repaired in 1725 by Gregorius Struve from Bremen. The year 1860 brought J. C. Schmid to St. Johannes for repairs and the addition of a two-stop, independent Pedal. In 1914 yet another Schnitger organ suffered at the hands of J. M. Schmid, when a new organ was installed and all but several rows of Schnitger pipes and the old Prospekt were discarded. The Schnitger Prospekt was also preserved in a new 1968 installation by Bosch-Sandershauser of Kassel.

Ganderkesee: St. Cornelius und Cyprianus

The 1699 Schnitger contract read

> Specification of the stops of an organ which could suitably fit the church at Ganderkesee.[5]

In the Manual		*In the Brustwerk*	
1. Principal	8′	1. Gedact very lovely	8′
2. Quintadena	16′		
3. Rohrfloit	8′	2. Blockfloit of wood	4′
4. Octav	4′		
5. Super Octav	2′	3. Spitzfloit	2′
6. Waltfloit	2′	4. Octav	2′
7. Sexquialt	2f.	5. Sieflit	1½′
8. Quint	1½′	6. Scharf	3f.
9. Mixtur	4f.		
10. Trommet	8′	Tremulant	

Total 16 stops, with 2 wind-chests on which the above listed stops are to stand, two manuals from C to c''', in all 45 keys, a suspended Pedal, three bellows 8 feet long, 4 feet wide, of good dry oak wood with the channels and wind pipes; the metal of the pipes shall be specified at 1000 lbs. lead and 300 lbs. tin. All the attachments and springs of brass, the structure with two doors, together with all the decorations according to the attached sketch, of good oak wood. All this shall be of good material, and the work shall be honestly done, so that when it is delivered nothing about it is faulty; the church builds the foundation with the two steps and the railing, has the materials brought from Bremen by wagon and, while the work is in progress, provides a house and heating and has nothing further to do.

On the signing of this contract fifty Reichsthaler are to be paid. When the organ works arrive, likewise 50 Reichsthaler.

When the work is finished and has been delivered without fault, the remainder, which is still due, is 380 Reichsthaler. Arp Schnitger binds himself, when the organ is finished and has been examined by impartial men, that the organ shall be found to be worth 50 Reichsthaler more than is paid for it. Further, Master Builder Arp Schnitger obligates himself to begin immediately on the work, so that on Midsummer Day of this year 1699 the work can be brought from Bremen, in order that it may be delivered finished by Martin Mass of the same year.

Executed at Delmenhorst, the 19 April 1699

	J. BORNHOLT	ARP SCHNITGER
VON WITZLEBEN	Pastor	Organ Builder
HINRICH WAGNER [?]	MENKE VOSTIN [?]	DIRK FOSTER [?]

That the 50 Reichsthaler, which are named in this contract, have been duly paid to me at the signing, is hereby acknowledged and receipt for it duly given.

ARP SCHNITGER

Schnitger's pride in his reputation and workmanship asserted itself in negotiations with the church officials at Ganderkesee when they balked at paying the customary one-third at the time of signing the contract. They wished to make two payments of 50 Rtl. and withhold the balance of 380 Rtl. until the inspection had been completed. This miserly attitude caused Schnitger to write the final paragraph into the contract. In view of the fact that Schnitger had been honored by the Danish king in February of the same year for his supremacy in the profession, the Ganderkesee insult was even more ridiculous. Pride notwithstanding, Schnitger proceeded with the project while simultaneously engaged in building four large organs in Magdeburg, Buxtehude, and Clausthal-Zellerfeld as well as smaller ones in Groningen (the Netherlands), Kloster Berge, and Dargun. The Uithuizen (the Netherlands) proposal was in progress during this period also.

There must have been quite a celebration on the occasion of the Ganderkesee dedication, for the cost of entertaining the guests was 21 Rtl. When the church wardens were asked by the consistory to give an itemized account so that Pastor Bornholt might be reimbursed for this amount, they replied:

> The reason that 21 Rtl. was spent on the occasion of such delivery is that the guests have consumed much and stayed long. Since the congregation has by now collected a large fund of 700 Rtl. for this construction, we feel confident that no one will expect the pastor to be hurt financially for the purposes of entertaining.[6]

Schnitger was not to share in the excess funds, however, as is confirmed by this addendum to the contract:[7]

> After the best and faultless delivery of this organ today, the balance of monies of my contract have been fully and correctly paid with 430 Reichsthaler; this I acknowledge in the best way by giving a correct receipt herewith. I promise besides that whatever within one year in the way of tuning and other defects in the aforesaid organ should result from the organ itself and not from lack of care, these I will myself, under the above sum, repair at my own expense; however,

> that free meals will be provided for me by the church and ten Reichsthaler be given me for my labor and materials for the present retuning of the organ pipes, the just payment according to the contract.
>
> Ganderkesee, 16 October 1699
> ARP SCHNITGER
> Organ Builder

The organ consisted of 16 voices with suspended Pedal and was erected on a new west balcony. Schnitger furnished the case work and ornaments himself, and his name is still legible thereon. In 1760, J. H. Klapmeyer of Oldenburg added a free-standing Pedal with six voices in two side towers. It boasted Prinzipal 8′, Oktave 4′, Mixtur 4f., Posaune 16′, Trompete 8′, and Trompete 4′, with the Prinzipal 8′ serving as frontal pipes. J. G. Schmid of Oldenburg, who completely overhauled the organ for 400 Rtl. in 1819, remarked that "the organ was built by the famous Arp Schnitger from Hamburg well and conscientiously in the style of his time, creating a distinctive effect in the large and venerable building; however, when being played, the indispensible Subbass 16′ is missing in the Pedal."[8] Even so, Schnitger's work remained unaltered until 1890, when J. M. Schmid of Oldenburg undertook "improvements." The bellows and channels had been replaced in 1868 by J. C. Schmid. Alfred Führer of Wilhelmshaven carried out extensive renovations in several stages from 1934 to 1966, which resulted in the present specifications.[9]

Alfred Führer (died 1975) drew the fire of numerous experts in the field of organ building when he divulged that the Rohrflöte 8′ in the main division was nothing more than a Gedackt with a soldered chimney. Schnitger had submitted specifications including a Rohrflöte prior to construction of the organ, but changed his mind and installed a Gedackt 8′, possibly because the latter was more suitable for the acoustical situation. The church officials did not concur with the change, and to satisfy them, Schnitger merely soldered a chimney to

St. Cornelius und Cyprianus, Ganderkesee

Hauptwerk (Manual I)

Quintadena	16′	Schnitger
Prinzipal	8′	Schnitger, in Prospekt
Rohrflöte	8′	Schnitger
Oktave	4′	Schnitger
Super Oktave	2′	Schnitger
Waldflöte	2′	Führer, 1966
Quinte	1⅓′	Führer, 1966
Sesquialtera	2f.	Schnitger C–h°; remainder, Führer, 1934
Mixtur	4f.	Führer, 1966
Trompete	8′	Giesecke, 1966

Brustwerk (Manual II)

Gedackt	8′	Schnitger
Blockflöte	4′	Schnitger, C–H stopped, remainder open
Oktave	2′	Führer, 1966
Spitzflöte	2′	Schnitger, conical
Sifflöte	1⅓′	Führer, 1966
Scharff	3f.	Führer, 1966

Pedal

Subbass	16′	Führer, 1934
Prinzipal	8′	Klapmeyer, in Prospekt
Oktave	4′	Klapmeyer; some pipes new in 1966
Posaune	16′	Boots and tongues, Schmid
Trompete	8 ′	Giesecke, 1966
Trompete	4′	Giesecke, 1966

Tremulant
Pitch: about ½ tone above normal
Wind Pressure: 72 mm

the Gedackt so that the pipes looked like Rohrflöten, thus appeasing the officials. Evidently he fooled a number of people for some 235 years!

The church at Ganderkesee is located in the loveliest of

settings. The yard is beautifully landscaped and filled with flowers and large evergreens. The interior is rather stark, the extremely high windows let in little light, and the altar area is relatively plain, all of which tend to direct one's attention to the commanding organ in its salmon pink case.

Rastede: St. Ulrich

The Benedictine Cloister of Rastede reported repairs to an organ as early as 1375, the oldest records relevant to an organ in the Oldenburg jurisdiction. St. Ulrich's, the town church with which Schnitger later contracted, suffered the collapse of its roof in 1695, at which time its organ was extensively damaged. Under orders from the Oldenburg Consistory, Arp Schnitger examined the instrument on July 14, 1709 and submitted the following report to which was appended the subsequent contract with the church:[10]

> By order of the Most Praiseworthy Royal Consistory in Oldenburg, I, the undersigned, went to Rastede, as arranged with the Very Reverend Pastor of that city, and have examined, in the presence of Herr Wichardt, organist in Oldenburg, the church and the old organ and found that the old works are completely destroyed and good for nothing, except that the small bellows are only worth 10 Reichsthaler. The old pipe work is pure lead; if this is melted and weighed, it could be of value. The rest is worn out from age, broken to pieces and can be used for nothing but to be burned, to which the above-mentioned Herr Pastor and Herr Wichardt, who have examined it with me, can bear witness. However, it would be well that in the aforesaid church, for the same large and populous parish, a completely new instrument should be placed on the western side by the tower, with the following stops, as

Upper Manual

1. Principal	4′		45 pipes
2. Floite dues	8′	(from wood)	45 pipes

3.	Octav	2′	45 pipes
4.	Sexquialt	2f.	90 pipes
5.	Quinta	1½′	45 pipes

Lower Manual

6.	Gedact	8′	45 pipes
7.	Floit	4′	45 pipes
8.	Nassat	3′	45 pipes
9.	Octav	2′	45 pipes
10.	Waltfloit	2′	45 pipes
11.	Mixtur	4f.	180 pipes
12.	Trompet	8′	45 pipes
		Total	720 pipes

In addition, a double wind-chest of the best heartwood where the aforementioned stops are to be placed, two manuals of beech with the semitones of ebony, a pedalboard with coupler such that both manuals can be used at the same time and also that the Pedal can be used with both manuals. Further, three bellows, 7 feet long and 3½ feet wide, together with new registers [stop knobs], trackers and channels [wind ducts], all appendages, springs and tuning wires of brass. In addition, the organ builder furnishes the instrument with carving, woodwork, and wrought-iron work, all the materials necessary for the above-mentioned organ building, and has the work executed honestly in all details, which, after careful consideration of the material and of the compensation for the work, costs 325 Reichsthaler.

There will be some changes in the foundation and pews of the church, which will have the finished articles brought from Elsfleth, to which place the organ builder himself, at his own risk and costs, will give, during the erection and tuning, food and drink, heat and light, and keep during that period an assistant, which brings the presentation of my humble services to the Reverend Royal Consistory: given at

Rastede, 14 June 1709
I remain your humble, obedient servant
ARP SCHNITGER

The organ builder Arp Schnitger agrees to manufacture all that which has been set forth above and to speed up the work in such a fashion that, God willing, it will be delivered finished; however, it is agreed that for the 1½′ Quinta, one of 3 feet shall be substituted and that the great F♯ and G♯ shall be introduced to all the stops, and also in the manuals and Pedal. In return, the Right Reverend Pastor and Magistrate of the said church promise the organ builder the payment of 285 Reichsthaler, but with the provision that this contract is approved by the High Praiseworthy Consistory in Oldenburg beforehand.

Also, the little that still remains of the old positiv (the old pipes have now been weighed and are not fully 200 pounds in weight so at the most cannot be valued at more than 5 Reichsthaler); when, however, the organ builder observes the bad condition of the church and other original equipment, he is satisfied with the above-mentioned 285 Reichsthalers together with what remains of the old instrument, to be paid in two installments, the first 100 Reichsthaler when this contract is approved, the remaining 185 Reichsthaler when everything has been well and satisfactorily delivered; this to be sworn by both parties to the contract; this agreement has been executed and signed in the name of God.

Rastede, 14 June 1709

Arp Schnitger	A. Maes, Pastor
Organ builder	Otto Philip
Wichardt	Hinrich Brattke [?]
Witness	

With the assistance of Schnitger's journeyman Johann Adam Gundermann, the organ was installed in the west gallery of the church near the close of 1709. According to the contract, Schnitger received 285 Rtl. and what remained of the old organ. In 1734 Johann Dietrich Busch of Itzehoe concluded a contract with the parish for repairs amounting to 65 Rtl. and the addition of an independent Pedal with Subbass 16′, Gedackt 8′, Octave 4′, and Trompete 8′ and 4′ costing 130 Rtl. Kraemershoff made minor repairs in 1803, and J. G. Schmid in

1833. The Schnitger organ was replaced by a new J. C. Schmid instrument in 1870-71. This organ was rebuilt in 1951 by the Alfred Führer Orgelbau and replaced in 1970 by a new Alfred Führer organ.

The Rastede and Leer organs were the last of the small Schnitgers. A return to Schnitger's concepts of design, scaling, and voicing in mechanical-action organs of two manual divisions with suspended or small independent Pedal may well extend the master builder's impact into a fifth century. With the current increase in the use of other instruments for worship services and concerts of sacred music, such organs, designed primarily for congregational support and continuo work, could be the twenty-first-century solution to the conflict between aesthetics and economics in parish churches, in the shrinking inner-city congregations, and in new, multipurpose suburban church buildings.

In considering the importance of the Schnitger legacy, there is no finer testimonial to the man or his organs than that of the Aurich organist Hermannus Schmit. On January 25, 1688 his opinion of Schnitger's St. Ludgeri organ in Norden concluded with these words:

> The work has been executed throughout with great industry, so that it will be rare in this country to find such perfect and artistic work, which must be said in honor of the organ builder.[11]

66. Organ at St. Laurentius, Dedesdorf. Schnitger, 1697–98.

St. Laurentius, Dedesdorf. 67. Manuals, stops, and pedalboard. 68. Trompete 8′, with Mixtur behind. *Opposite:* 69. Reconstructed tracker action, Alfred Führer Orgelbau, 1978. 70. Reconstructed wind reservoir, Führer, 1957.

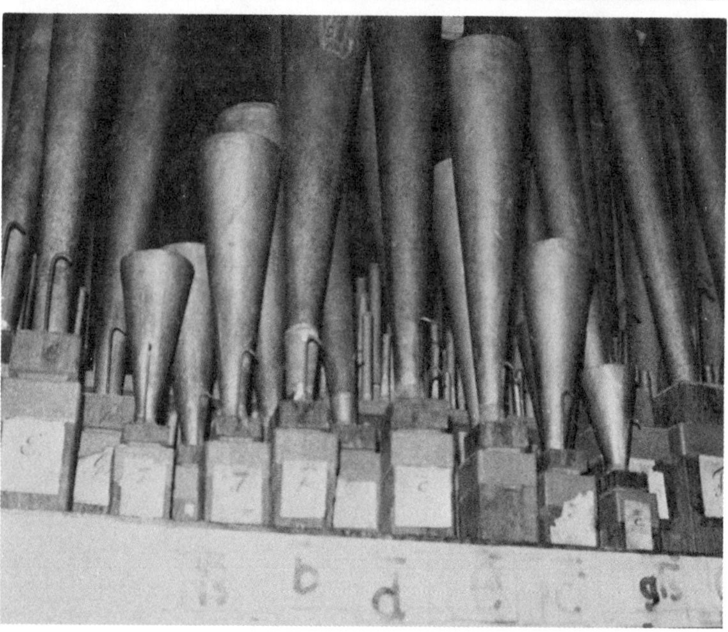

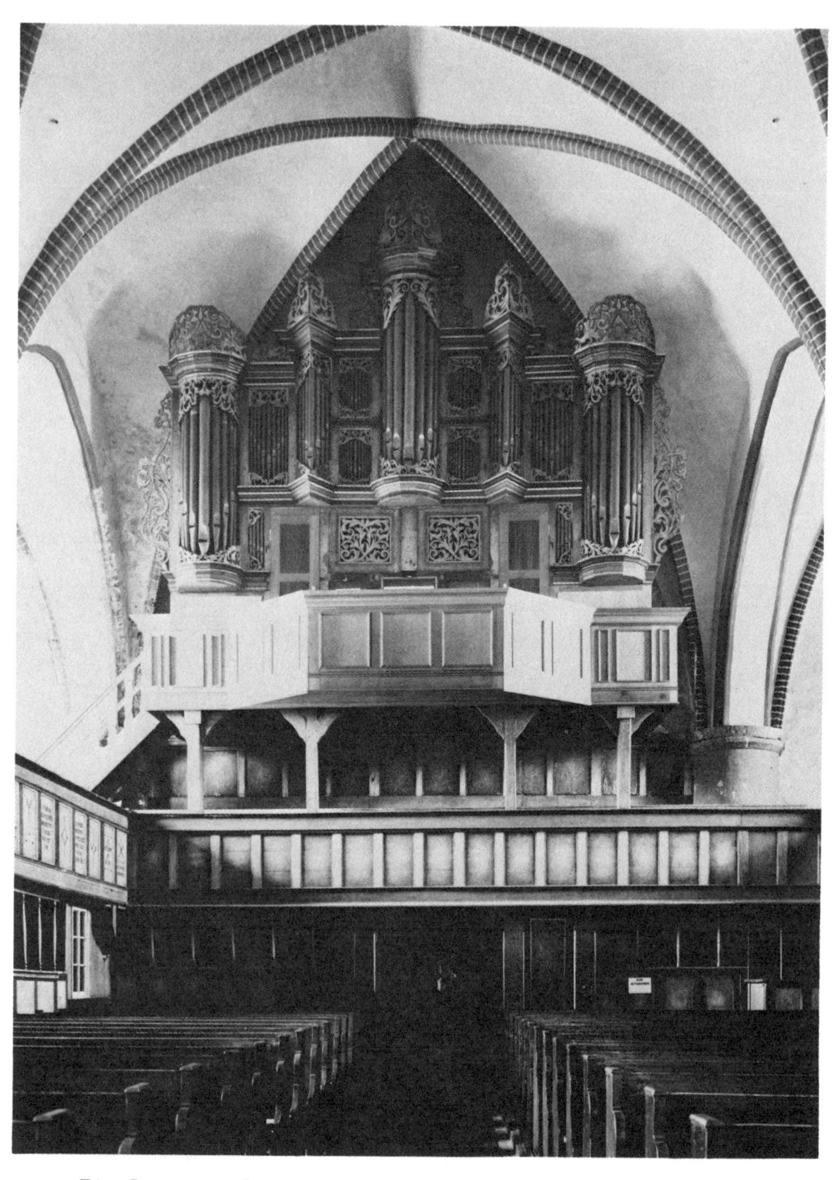

71. Organ at St. Cornelius und Cyprianus, Ganderkesee. Schnitger, 1699.

Appendix A

Chronological Listing of Schnitger's Organ Projects

(Originally Compiled by Gustav Fock)

1.	1676–78	New	Stade, St. Wilhadi, III+P/45. Prospekt and much pipe work from Bielfeldt's 1730–35 installation preserved.
2.	1677	Repair	Freiburg/Niederelbe, II+P/? Some old registers preserved.
3.	1677	Repair	Stade, St. Nikolai, III+P/33. RP-Prospekt in Kirchlinteln, near Verden, preserved; many older registers from the sixteenth century preserved in Himmelpforten, near Stade.
4.	1677	Repair	Borstel/Altes Land, II+P/? Prospekt from 1770–72 and much of sixteenth-century organ preserved.
5.	1678	Repair	Assel (near Stade), II+P/?
6.	1678	New	Scharmbeck (near Bremen), I/? Prospekt and majority of pipe work from 1731–34 installation by Bielfeldt preserved.
7.	1678–79	Rebuild	Jork/Altes Land, III+P/35. Prospekt preserved.
8.	1678–82	New	Oederquart (near Stade), III+P/28. Prospekt preserved.
9.	1679	New	Bülkau/Niederelbe, II+P/? Prospekt preserved.

10.	1680	New	Hamburg, St. Johannis-Klosterkirche, II+P/30. Today in Cappel, near Bremerhaven; Prospekt and pipe work almost completely preserved.
11.	1680	New	Hamburg-Nienstedten, I/?
12.	1680	Repair	Osten/Niederelbe, ?/? Prospekt from 1751 installation by J. Albrecht preserved.
13.	1680	Repair	Oldenburg, St. Lamberti, III+P/?
14.	1681	Rebuild	Hamburg-Kirchwerder, II+P/? Prospekt from 1784–86 and some old registers preserved.
15.	1682–83	New	Lüdingworth, near Cuxhaven, III+P/35. Prospekt and pipe work almost completely preserved.
16.	1682–87	New	Hamburg, St. Nikolai, IV+P/67. Destroyed in the 1842 Hamburg fire.
17.	1682–88	New	Hamburg-Neuenfelde, II+P/34. Prospekt and much pipe work preserved.
18.	1683–85	New	Schwei/Oldenburg, II/14.
19.	1684	New	Wittmund/Ostfriesland, II+P/? Prospekt from 1775 installation by H. J. Müller preserved.
20.	1684	New	Elmshorn/Holstein, II+P/23. Completion of work begun by J. Richborn.
21.	1685	Rebuild	Selsingen (near Stade), II+P/?
22.	1685–86	Repair	Hamburg, St. Katharinen, Chorpositiv, I/?
23.	1685–87	New	Steinkirchen/Altes Land, II+P/28. Prospekt and pipe work almost completely preserved.
24.	1686	Repair	Hamburg, Pesthofkirche, ?/?
25.	1686–87	New	Hamburg-Altona, Reformiert Kirche, II/?
26.	1686–88	New	Norden/Ostfriesland, IV+P/46. Prospekt and much pipe work preserved.
27.	1687	Rebuild	Hamburg, St. Pauli, ?/?
28.	1688	Rebuild	Mittelnkirchen/Altes Land, II+P/21. Prospekt from 1753 and many old registers preserved.
29.	1688	Rebuild	Stade, St. Cosmae, III+P/43. Prospekt and much of Huss's and Schnitger's work preserved.
30.	1688–89	Rebuild	Stade, St. Pankratius (Burgkirche), II+P/?
31.	1688–90	New	Hollern/Altes Land, II+P/24. Prospekt and part of pipe work preserved.

32.	1689–93	New	Hamburg, St. Jacobi, IV+P/60. Pipe material largely preserved.
33.	1689–95	New	Magdeburg, St. Johannis, III+P/62.
34.	1690	New	England, "small organ," ?/?
35.	1690	New	Hamburg, Residence organ for Dr. Hinckelmann, II/16.
36.	1691	New	Hamburg, St. Jacobi, Chancel positiv, I/?
37.	1691	New	Moscow, Residence organ for the Grand Duke, later Peter the Great.
38.	1691	Repair	Hamburg, St. Maria-Magdalene, II+P/23.
39.	1691–92	New	Lamstedt (near Stade), II+P/21.
40.	1691–92	Rebuild	Groningen, Martinikerk, III+P/39. Prospekt (Pedal pipes) and much pipe work preserved.
41.	1691	Repair	Delfzijl/Province Groningen, ?/?
42.	1692	Rebuild	Hamburg, St. Petri, IV+P/53.
43.	1692	Repair	Uithuizermeeden/Province Groningen, ?/?
44.	1693	New	Eutin/Holstein, Schlosskirche, II/? Prospekt preserved.
45.	1693	New	Gross-Ottersleben (near Magdeburg), II+P/?
46.	1693	New	Hagelberg (near Belzig/Brandenburg), I/6.
47.	1693	New	Hamburg, Residence organ for Alderman C. Anckelmann, I/8.
48.	1693	Rebuild	Groningen, Pelster-Gasthuiskerk, II/? Prospekt and part of pipe work preserved.
49.	1693–94	New	Hamburg, Waisenhaus, II+P/21. Today in Grasberg, near Bremen; Prospekt and much pipe work preserved.
50.	1693–96	Rebuild	Verden, Dom, II+P/25.
51.	1693–98	New	Bremen, Dom, III+P/30.
52.	1694	New	Hamburg-Hamm, Dreifaltigkeitskirche, II+P/20.
53.	1694	New	Kirche of "Jonkheer Poteck" (?), ?/?
54.	1694	New	Stade, Residence organ for General-Superintendant Dieckmann, II/?
55.	1694	New	Hamburg, Residence organ for Chief Clergyman Joh. Friedr. Mayer, I/8.
56.	1694–95	New	Sittensen (near Stade), II/13.
57.	1694–97	New	Groningen, Aa-Kerk, IV+P/40.
58.	1694–98	New	Magdeburg, Heilige-Geist-Kirche, II+P/26.
59.	1695	New	Groningen, Collegium Musicum, I/6.
60.	1695	New	Hamburg-Moorburg, I+P/13.

61.	1695	New	Middelstum/Province Groningen, II/15.
62.	1695	New	Nieuw Scheemda/Province Groningen, I/8. Prospekt and majority of pipe work preserved; only Schnitger organ remaining with original unequal temperament.
63.	1695	New	Den Haag, Residence organ for Herrn Gebhard, ?/?
64.	1695	New	Groningen, Residence organ for a cantor, ?/?
65.	1695	Repair	Noordwolde/Province Groningen, III+P/27. Prospekt from 1640 and many older registers preserved.
66.	1695	Repair	Zeerjip/Province Groningen, II+P/18. Prospekt from 1651 preserved.
67.	1695–96	New	Harkstede/Province Groningen, I/8. Prospekt and part of pipe work preserved.
68.	1695–96	New	Noordbroek/Province Groningen, II+P/20. Prospekt and much pipe work preserved.
69.	1695–98	New	Bremen, St. Stephani, III+P/42.
70.	1695–99	New	Achim (near Bremen), II+P/22.
71.	1696–97	New	Oldenbrok/Oldenburg, II/12. Prospekt from 1752–54 preserved.
72.	1696–97	Rebuild	Groningen, Gertruids-Gasthuiskerk, II+P/? Today in Peize.
73.	1696–98	New	Pieterburen/Province Groningen, I/8. Today in Mensingeweer/ Province Groningen; parts of Prospekt in both locations; much pipe work preserved.
74.	1696–99	New	Lübeck, Dom, III+P/45.
75.	1697	New	Moscow, Residence organ for Herrn Ernhorn, I/8.
76.	1697–98	Rebuild	Golzwarden/Oldenburg, II+P/20. Prospekt preserved.
77.	1697–98	New	Dedesdorf (near Bremerhaven), II/12. Prospekt and pipe work almost completely preserved.
78.	1697–98	New	Strückhausen, formally Altenkirchen/Oldenburg, II/12. Prospekt preserved.
79.	1697–98	Repair	Ratzeburg, Dom, III+P/?
80.	1698	New	Stade, Residence organ for the Chief Inspector, I/8.

81.	1698	New	Stade, Residence organ for Superintendent S. Baldovius, ?/?
82.	1698–99	New	Stettin, St. Jakobi, III+P/47. Completion of work begun by M. Schurig.
83.	1698–1700	New	Magdeburg, St. Ulrich, III+P/48.
84.	1698–1700	Rebuild	Bremen, Liebfrauenkirche, III+P/40.
85.	1698–1703	New	Magdeburg, St. Jakobi, III+P/37. Completion of work begun by H. Herbst.
86.	1699	New	Ganderkesee/Oldenburg, II/16. Prospekt and part of pipe work preserved.
87.	1699	New	Groningen, Lutherse Kerk, II/16.
88.	1699	Rebuild	Magdeburg, St. Petri, II P/?
89.	1699	New	Magdeburg-Kloster Berge, I+P/13.
90.	1699	Repair	Hamburg-Steinbeck, ?/?
91.	1699–1700	New	Dargun/Mecklenburg, Schlosskirche, II+P/22.
92.	1699–1700	Rebuild	Hamburg, St. Gertrud, II+P/21.
93.	1699–1700	Rebuild	Oldenburg, St. Lamberti, III+P/?
94.	1699–1701	New	Buxtehude, St. Petri, III+P/36.
95.	1699–1702	New	Clausthal-Zellerfeld, St. Salvatoris, III+P/55. Prospekt preserved.
96.	1700–1701	New	Uithuizen/Province Groningen, II+P/28. Prospekt and pipe work largely preserved.
97.	1700–1702	New	Groningen, Academiekerk, III+P/33; Today in the Aa-Kerk in Groningen; Prospekt and pipe work largely preserved.
98.	1700	New	Hamburg-Eppendorf, St. Johannis, II/11.
99.	1701	Repair	Hamburg, Dom, II+P/31.
100.	1701	Repair	Hamburg, St. Nikolai, III+P/27.
101.			Unidentified.
102.	1701	New	Portugal, two small organs, II/12.
103.	1701	Repair	Siddeburen/Province Groningen, I/10.
104.	1701–1702	New	Sandesneben/Lauenburg, II/15.
105.	1702	New	Estebrügge/Altes Land, II+P/34. Prospekt preserved.
106.	1702	Repair	Hamburg, Heilige-Geist-Hospital, II+P/27. Today in Cuxhaven-Ritzebüttel; pipe work partially preserved.
107.	1702	Repair	Ratzeburg, Stadtkirche, II+P/19.
108.	1702	Repair	Clausthal-Zellerfeld, St. Salvatoris, Positiv.
109.	1702–1703	Rebuild	Hamburg-Altona, Hauptkirche, II+P/?

110.	After 1702	New	Kiel, Schlosskapelle, II/19.
111.			Unidentified.
112.			Unidentified.
113.	After 1702	New	Bremen, three Residence organs.
114.	After 1702	New	Spain, small organ ?/?
115.	After 1702	New	Harkstede/Province Groningen, Residence organ for Herrn Piccardt, ?/?
116.	1703–1705	Repair	Burhave/Oldenburg, II/?
117.	1703–1705	Rebuild	Eckwarden/Oldenburg, II/17.
118.	1704	New	Godlinze/Province Groningen, I/10. Prospekt and pipe material almost completely preserved.
119.	1704	New	Eenum/Province Groningen, I/10. Prospekt and part of pipe work preserved.
120.	1704	New	Eexta/Province Groningen, I/? Prospekt preserved.
121.	1704	Repair	Irnsum/Province Friesland, I/?
122.	1704–1705	Rebuild	Langwarden/Oldenburg, II+P/21. Prospekt from 1650 and many old registers preserved.
123.	1704–1705	New	Esenshamm/Oldenburg, II/16.
124.	1704–1705	Rebuild	Langenweddingen (near Magdeburg), ?/?
125.	1704–1705	Repair	Jade/Oldenburg, I/11. Prospekt and part of pipe work from 1737–39 installation by J. D. Busch preserved.
126.	1704–1705	Repair	Twielenfleth/Altes Land, I/8.
127.	1705	New	Accum/Oldenburg, II/? Prospekt preserved.
128.	1705	New	Neuenkirchen/Norderdithmarschen, II+P/24.
129.	1705	Repair	Hammelwarden/Oldenburg, I/?
130.	1705	Repair	Rodenkirchen/Oldenburg, II/?
131.	1705–1706	Repair	Elsfleth/Oldenburg, I/6.
132.	1705–1706	Rebuild	Magdeburg, St. Katharinen, I/?
133.	1705–1707	Rebuild	Stollhamm/Oldenburg, II+P/24.
134.	1706	New	Berlin-Charlottenburg, Schlosskapelle, II+P/26.
135.			Unidentified.
136.			Unidentified.
137.			Unidentified.
138.	1706–1710	Maintenance	Berlin, Dom; Königl. Schloss; Schlosskapelle Oranienburg and Potsdam
139.	c.1706	New	Magdeburg-Neustadt, Nonnenkloster, ?/?
140.	1706–1708	New	Berlin, St. Nikolai, III+P/40.

141.	1706–1707	New	Berlin, St. Sebastian, II+P/24.
142.	1707–1708	New	Hamburg-Ochsenwerder, II+P/30. Prospekt and one register preserved.
143.	1707–1709	Rebuild	Flensburg, St. Nikolai, III+P/42. Prospekt from 1604 preserved.
144.	1707–1709	Rebuild	Bremen, St. Martini, II+P/26. Prospekt from 1615 preserved.
145.	1708–1709	New	Beverstedt (near Bremerhaven), II/18. One pre-Schnitger register preserved.
146.	1709	New	Rastede/Oldenburg, II/12.
147.	1709–10	New	Lunsen (near Bremen), II/20.
148.	1709–10	New	Weener/Ostfriesland, I/22. Prospekt and one register preserved.
149.	1709–11	Rebuild	Delmenhorst/Oldenburg, II+P/?
150.	1710	Rebuild	Bernau (near Berlin), III+P/38.
151.	1710–11	New	Sneek/Province Friesland, Martinikerk, III+P/36. Prospekt and one register preserved.
152.	1710–13	New	Abbehausen/Oldenburg, II+P/24. Prospekt preserved.
153.	1711	New	Ferwerd/Province Friesland, II+P/26.
154.	1711	New	Nordsee-Insel Pellworm, Alte Kirche, II+P/24. Prospekt and part of pipe work preserved.
155.	1712	New	Leeuwarden, Lutherse Kerk, I+P/15.
156.	1712–13	Rebuild	Waddens/Oldenburg, II/10.
157.	1712–15	New	Hamburg, St. Michaelis, III+P/52. Destroyed by lightning in 1750.
158.	1712-15	Repair	Oldenburg, St. Lamberti, III+P/?
159.	After 1712	New	Hamburg, Residence organ for Frau Fittsche, ?/?
160.	After 1712	New	Hamburg, Residence organ for Herrn Koppesohn, ?/?
161.	1713–14	New	Leer/Ostfriesland, Luther Kirche, II/18?
162.	1713–14	Repair	Stade, St. Wilhadi. Restoration following Danish bombardment, which had damaged the organ.
163.	1714–16	New	Rendsburg, Christkirche, II+P/29. Prospekt preserved.
164.	1714–18(?)	Rebuild	Bremen, St. Ansgari, III+P/? Prospekt preserved.
165.	1715	New	Osternburg/Oldenburg, I/6.
166.	1715–19	New	Itzehoe/Holstein, St. Laurentius, III+P/43. Incomplete; Prospekt preserved.

167.	c.1716	New	Itzehoe, Residence organ for a judge, ?/?
168.	1718	New	Bremen, St. Pauli, ?/?
169.	1718	New	Zwolle, Grote of Michaelskerk, III+P/46. Planned by Schnitger and completed by Franz Caspar and Johann Jürgen Schnitger, 1719–21; Prospekt and much pipe work preserved.

Appendix B

Scalings for Representative Schnitger Organs

Scalings for the Schnitger Organ at Nieuw Scheemda by Orgelbauer Metzler & Söhne, Zurich

	C	c°	c'	c''	c'''
1. Praestant 4′					
Diameter	85.5	47.4	27.0	17.4	11.2
Mouth	59.7	36.3	19.7	12.7	8.8
Cut-up	15.7	9.8	5.5	3.6	2.5
2. Holpijp 8′					
Diameter	97.8	54.0	32.1	21.9	16.7
Mouth	73.1	41.4	25.2	17.6	13.8
Cut-up	24.4	18.0	11.5	7.7	4.6
3. Fluit 4′					
Diameter	64.5	43.0	29.8	18.2	11.1
Mouth	49.4	33.8	30.2	15.0	9.2
Cut-up	19.0	11.3	7.9	3.9	2.3
4. Quint 3′					
Diameter	59.0	31.8	17.6	12.2	7.4
Mouth	45.2	26.3	14.5	10.4	6.3
Cut-up	15.1	8.8	3.9	2.8	1.6

5. Octaaf 2′

Diameter	45.0	24.0	15.5	9.8	8.0
Mouth	34.5	20.3	12.2	9.6	6.1
Cut-up	9.8	7.0	4.2	3.1	2.0

6. Quintadena 8′ (Treble)

Diameter			30.9	20.6	12.8
Mouth			23.7	16.2	10.0
Cut-up			6.8	4.5	2.7

7. Mixtuur III f. (½′)

2⅔				12.0	8.1
2			15.9	9.8	6.9
1⅓			12.0	7.9	4.9
1		15.9	9.8		
⅔		12.0			
½	15.9	9.8			
⅓	12.0				
¼	9.8				

8. Trompet 8′

Resonator length	176 cm	88 cm	44 cm	19.7 cm	5.4 cm
Top diameter (mm)	97.8	65.0	52.0	47.0	42.5
Bottom diameter	21.0	16.3	12.8	10.0	8.1
Tongue thickness	0.49	0.37	0.30	0.20	0.13

Scalings for the Schnitger Organ at Dedesdorf by Alfred Führer Orgelbau, Wilhelmshaven

a = Diameter
b = Mouth
c = Cut-up
d = Length
e = Length of foot
f = Toe hole
g = Languid thickness
h = Wall thickness at top
i = Wall thickness at bottom
j = Ears
k = Upper pipe edge
1. Mostly closed
2. Slightly closed
3. Normal
4. Open
5. Wide open or with tuning roll

n = New
x = Soldered in
+ = Soldered on

Pitch Level: approximately ¾ of a half-tone above normal
Wind Pressure: 70 mm WS

MANUAL

1. Quintadena 8′

	C	c°	c'	c''	c'''
a	92	51.6	29.5	20	15.8
b	70	40	20	14.5	11.5
c	23	13	8	5	3.5
d	1102	550	270	127	56
e	215	196	192	195	195
f	11.5	7.5	7.0	6.2	5.0
g	3	2.5	1.5	1.2	1.0
h	0.65	0.55	0.4	0.6	0.3
i	0.9	0.7			
j	72×23	42×22	34×11	25×15	20×9.5

Leathered caps
Round mouth: C–b°

2. Flöte 4′

	C	c°	c'	c''	c'''
a	63.5	40.7	26.6	19.2	16.5
b	48.5	32	20	16	12
c	21	12.5	8.5	4.5	2.8
d	530	252	177	53	19
e	170	152	148	149	147
f	8.5n	7.0	7.2	7.0	5.5n
g	4.5	2.8	2.2	1.2	1.2
i	0.55	0.55			
j	57×25	39×18	31×15	20×11	16×8

Soldered pipes (for permanent tuning)
Round mouth: c–f°
Pressed-in mouth: f#–c'''

3. Quinte 3′

	C	c°	c'	c''	c'''
a	55.5	30.3	16.6	10.5	6.5
b	42	22	13	7.0	5.0
c	12.2	7.8	4.5	1.8	2.0
d	733	368	185	88	45.5
e	192	147	146	146	146
f	7.5	7.5	5.5	5.0	5.5
g	4.0	2.0	1.0	1.0	1.0
h	0.9	0.5	0.6	0.8	0.5
i	0.9	0.8	0.8		
k		3	3	3	2

Some isolated ears
Tuning ears: C, G
Tuning rolls: E, F♯, G♯, B

4. Flöte 2′

	C	c°	c'	c''	c'''
a	53	22.5	14.8	9.2	5.8
b	40	17.2	12	8.0	4.5
c	10	6.2	3.6	2.5	1.8
d	540	276	136	66	32
e	177	146	146	145	142
f	7n	6.8	6.5	5.5	6.5
g	3.5	1.5	1.5	1.0	0.8
h	n	0.6	0.7	0.6	0.4
i	0.8	0.9	0.7		
k	5	3	3	2	2

Some isolated ears
Round Mouth: C–B
Tuning rolls: c°–a°

5. Gemshorn 2′

	C	c°	c'	c''	c'''
a, above	54.2	35.8	24.5	15.5	10.5
a, below	17.2	15.0	12.8	9.1	5.2
b	37	25	15	9	6

c	9.5	6.5	4.0	2.2	1.7
d	530	250	115	52	22
e	195	195	200	197	194
f	6.0	7.0	5.0	4.5	6.0n
g	2.5	1.8	1.2	1.0	0.8
h	0.8	0.9	0.5	0.4	0.4
i	0.8	0.6			
j	4	3	3	3	2

No ears
Pointed mouth: c–d♯°

6. Sesquialtera 2 ranks

C= 2/3′ + 2/5′
c°= 1 1/3′ + 4/5′
c'= 2 2/3′ + 1 3/5′

1st Rank

	C	c°	c'	c''	c'''
a	16.3	17.0	16.5	10.0	6.6
b	13.5	14.0	13.0	8.0	5.0
c	4.5	4.5	3.5	3.5	1.8
d	186	183	185	92	43
e	140	145	144	147	150
f	7.0	6.5	6.2	5.0	6.0
g	2.0	2.2	2.0	1.8	0.8
h	0.5	0.6	0.5	0.4	n
k	4	2	2	4	n

2nd Rank

	C	c°	c'	c''	c'''
a	11.0	11.0	11.2	8.0	5.8
b	8.0	8.0	8.2	6.2	4.5
c	3.5	3.0	2.8	2.2	1.4
d	109	110	110	53	24
e	147	147	138	146	148
f	6.2	6.0	4.5	6.5	6.0
g	1.5	1.5	1.8	1.2	0.8
h	0.4	0.5	0.6	0.5	0.4
k	3	2	2	2	2

7. Mixtur 4 ranks

C = 1/2′ + 1/3′ + 1/4′ + 1/4′
c° = 1′ + 2/3′ + 1/2′ + 1/2′
c' = 2′ + 1 1/3′ + 1′ + 1′
c'' = 2 2/3′ + 2′ + 1′ + 1′
d♯' = 2 2/3′ + 2′ + 1 3/5′ + 1 1/3′

1st Rank

	C	c°	c'	c''	c'''
a	12.2	12.3	12.6	10.0	7.2
b	10	9.5	10.0	7.5	5.5
c	3.6	3.8	3.2	2.2	1.8
d	139	140	136	82	44
e	145	145	146	143	148
f	6.0	5.5	5.5n	5.0n	5.5
g	1.5	1.8	1.8	1.3	1.0
h	0.5	0.6	0.5	0.7	0.6
k	2	2	2	1	2

2nd Rank

	C	c°	c'	c''	c'''
a	9.8	9.8	9.8	8.8	5.6
b	6.8	7.8	7.2	7.0	4.6
c	2.8	2.8	2.5	2.5	1.5
d	92	91	90	68	33
e	146	150	146	148	145
f	5.2n	5.2n	5.5	5.2n	5.5
g	1.5	1.5	1.2	1.5	1.0
h	0.6	n	0.5	0.5	0.4
k	2	2	2	2	3

3rd Rank

	C	c°	c'	c''	c'''
a	8.0	8.1	8.4	6.0	n
b	6.5	6.5	6.5	3.8	n
c	2.2	2.5	2.0	1.7	n
d	67	67	67.5	31	n
e	146	149	142	145	n
f	5.5	5.0n	5.0	5.5	n
g	1.5	1.5	1.5	1.2	n
h	0.5	0.4	0.5	0.5	n
k	1	2	3	2	n

New pipes from c'''

4th Rank

	C	c°	c'	c''	c'''
a	8.2	8.0	8.5	6.0	n
b	6.8	6.8	6.5	4.5	n
c	2.1	2.9	1.8	1.2	n
d	68	67.5	67	30	n
e	145	147	146	146	n
f	5.5	6.0	4.2n	6.0	n
g	1.2	1.2	1.2	1.2	n
h	0.5	0.4	0.6	0.5	n
k	2	2	3	3	n

New pipes from g''
Pressed-in mouths

8. Trompete 8′

Tongue (n)

	C	c°	c'	c''	c'''
Upper width	17.0	12.5	7.2	6.9	5.0
Lower width	20.1	14.2	9.0	7.8	6.3
Upper thickness	0.5	0.3	0.18	0.10	0.07
Lower thickness	0.5	0.3	0.18	0.10	0.07

Shallot

	C	c°	c'	c''	c'''
a	122	77	54	37	26
c	85	47	33		
d	11.8	5.5	6.2		
e	5.0	1.0	2.6		
f	22.4	18.0	13.6	8.5	7.1
g	20.9	16.0	12.2	7.7	6.0
h	23.2	17.2	13.6	7.2	6.5
i	19.7	15.0	11.8	7.5	5.8
j	5.2	4.0	2.2		
k	18.0	13.2	14.2	6.8	5.8
l	14.5	11.2	8.0	5.5	4.2

Lead plate: C–d♯'

Resonator

	C	c°	c'	c''(n)	c'''
a Top	129.5	102.0	75.0	62.0n	43.0
a Bottom	27.5	21.0	17.0	12.0n	15.0
d	1910	957	436	225n	72
h	1.0	0.68	0.7	0.6	0.8
i	1.9	1.2	0.8		

Boot

	C	c°	c'	c''	c'''
Width	73	59	45	42.5	37.5
Depth	66	49	40	35.5	30.5
Bore	10.8	7.5	9.0	8.5	7.0
Outer length	121	105	69	55	46
Inner length	134	119	80	67	59

Block

	C	c°	c'	c''	c'''
d	38	20	20	14	12
e	56	38	35	30	26
f	26	19	20	15	14
g	20	16	13	8.2	6.5
k	22	20	18	13	14
l	100	61	39	25	15
m	3.0	2.2	2.0	2.0	1.5
n	60	51	43	34	30
o	51	42	36	27	25

BRUSTWERK

1. Gedackt 8′

	C	c°	c'	c''	c'''
a	102.5	63	41	26.6	20
b	80	48.5	31	21	15
c	23.5x	19	11	7	4
d	1100	538	258	123	54
e	160	160	158	150	150
f	13	8	8.8	5.0	6.0

g	4.0	3.0	2.2	1.8	1.5
i	1.35	0.7	0.8		
j	86×36	58×20	36×17	35×16	26×13

Soldered
Round mouth: C–e'

2. Prinzipal 4′

	C	c°	c'	c''	c'''
a	83	49	28.5	17.5	10.8
b	62	38	21.5	12.5	7.5
c	14.5	9.0	5.5	3.0	1.8
h–i		0.6	0.6	0.5	0.4

New register by Alfred Führer, 1957, situated in the Prospekt
Tuning rolls
Pointed mouth

3. Oktav 2′

	C	c°	c'	c''	c'''
a	43.5	23.5	13.2	8.8	6.3
b	32	18	11	7.0	5.5
c	10.5	6.5	3.6x	2.8	2.0
d	556+	280+	140	67	32
e	144	142	147	146	146
f	7.2	5.0	5.0	5.5	6.5
g	3.5	1.2	1.7	1.0	0.8
h	0.5	0.6	0.6	0.3	0.4
i	0.8	0.6	0.6	0.3	0.3
k	5	5	2	2	4

Round mouth, C–B

4. Quinte 1⅓′

	C	c°	c'	c''	c'''
a	29.5	16.4	10	7	
b	24	13.5	8.5	5.5	
c	6.5	3.2x	3.5	2.2	

d	371+	186+	93	45
e	145	146	146	145
f	6.5	6.0	5.0	5.5
g	2.2	1.2	0.8	0.6
h	0.45		0.4	0.5
i	0.6	0.5	0.4	0.4
k	4	4	3	3

c'''–New
Round mouth, C–E

Scalings for the Schnitger Organ at Steinkirchen by Rudolf von Beckerath Orgelbau, Hamburg

Hauptwerk

	C	c°	c'	c''	c'''
1. Prinzipal 8′, in Prospekt					
Diameter	148.7	92.7	48.8	28.4	18.5
Mouth	112.6	68.0	35.8	19.6	12.8
Cut-up	25.7	18.5	10.8	6.2	4.3
2. Quintadena 16′, stopped; all pipes with ears, box-beards					
Diameter	151.5	96.0	54.0	34.5	22.5
Mouth	114.0	72.0	43.2	26.8	16.3
3. Rohrflöte 8′, stopped; all pipes with ears; from c°, capped					
Diameter	110.0	82.4	55.0	30.5	17.8
Mouth	81.8	57.5	39.8	21.4	11.0
Cut-up	38.0	25.0	13.5	7.8	5.8
Chimney					
Length		127.0	92.0	55.0	42.0
Diameter		20.0	15.3	12.2	7.4
Length of body		540.0	240.0	119.0	55.0
4. Oktave 4′, C–d° with ears					
Diameter	74.5	45.0	25.2	15.6	9.2
Mouth	55.0	35.0	18.8	11.5	6.0
Cut-up	22.0	13.0	7.8	5.0	3.2

5. Nasat 3′, conical

Lower diameter	76.2	60.0	42.2	23.0	new
Upper diameter	58.0	43.0	34.0	14.0	new
Mouth	50.0	36.0	26.8	12.8	new
Cut-up	23.0	13.5	6.8	4.5	new
Length of body	630.0	275.0	125.0	60.0	new

6. Oktave 2′, C–B with ears

Diameter	45.7	26.2	16.0	8.8	7.0
Mouth	30.6	19.0	11.0	5.8	4.3
Cut-up	14.5	8.2	5.8	3.0	2.2

7. Gemshorn 2′, cylindrical; C–c′ with ears

Diameter	58.5	36.0	25.5	16.0	12.2
Mouth	40.2	27.2	16.8	11.0	8.1
Cut-up	10.7	7.8	5.0	3.2	2.0

8. Sesquialtera 2 ranks

C = 1⅓′ + 4/5′
c° = 2⅔′ + 1 3/5′

	G1⅓′	G⅔′	G⅓′	G1/6′	C1/8′
Diameter	32.0	18.8	11.0	6.5	5.4
Mouth	24.8	13.5	7.0	4.2	3.3
Cut-up	7.2	5.3	3.0	2.0	1.8

9. Mixtur 4, 5, 6 ranks

C = 1′ + ⅔′ + ½′ + ⅓′
c° = 1⅓′ + 1′ + ⅔′ + ½′
c′ = 2′ + 1⅓′ + 1′ + ⅔′
c♯′ = 2′ + 1⅓′ + 1′ + ⅔′ + ⅔′
c″ = 4′ + 2⅔′ + 2′ + 2′ + 1⅓′ + 1⅓′

	C1′	C½′	C¼′	C⅛′
Diameter 1′	23.8	14.8	9.6	6.5
Mouth	17.7	11.0	6.9	4.3
Cut-up	7.8	4.9	3.1	2.1

10. Cimbel 3 ranks, von Beckerath, according to Schnitger disposition

C = 1/4′ + 1/5′ + 1/6′
c° = 1/2′ + 2/5′ + 1/3′
c' = 1′ + 4/5′ + 2/3′
c'' = 2′ + 1 3/5′ + 1 1/3′

11. Trompete 8′

	C	c°	c'	c''	c'''
Shallot					
Upper diameter	19.3	13.0	9.8	7.0	5.5
Lower diameter	14.8	12.0	7.5	5.5	4.5
Length	117.0	82.0	50.0	37.5	27.0
Resonator					
Diameter	120.0	85.0	62.0	46.0	41.0
Length	1905	861	457	217	100

BRUSTWERK

1. Gedackt 8′, C–G, oak by Schnitger; from A, oak by von Beckerath

	C	G	
Height	72.0	55.0	(remainder
Mouth	60.0	44.0	not
Cut-up	40.0	23.0	original)

2. Rohrflöte 4′

	C	c°	c'	c''	c'''
Diameter	64.0	41.5	26.8	19.3	13.2
Mouth	49.0	32.0	20.0	12.3	8.2
Cut-up	23.0	14.5	9.6	5.7	3.5
Chimney					
Length	168.0	84.0	46.5	30.0	14.0
Diameter	22.0	17.5	12.5	9.6	7.2
Length of body	594.0	301.0	154.0	64.0	27.0

3. Quinte 2⅔′, conical

Lower diameter	65.3	36.8	25.0	19.8	14.0
Upper diameter	20.5	13.2	11.0	10.0	8.8
Mouth	49.0	27.0	17.0	13.0	9.1
Cut-up	13.2	8.8	5.8	4.0	2.5
Length of body	693.0	340.0	162.0	71.0	38.0

4. Oktave 2′

Diameter	45.8	26.8	17.0	9.7	5.5
Mouth	34.0	18.5	11.7	6.5	3.2
Cut-up	11.7	8.2	4.1	3.6	2.0

5. Spitzflöte 2′, conical

Lower diameter	56.0	37.5	25.5	16.5	10.8
Upper diameter	19.0	13.5	9.5	8.0	7.5
Mouth	37.5	26.0	18.2	10.3	6.3
Cut-up	12.1	7.9	5.7	2.2	1.8
Length of body	497.0	227.0	108.0	44.0	19.0

6. Tertian 2 ranks

C = 1⅗′ + 1⅓′

Diameter	35.6	new	12.3	7.7	5.0
Mouth	27.5	new	8.8	5.9	3.2
Cut-up	7.8	new	3.3	2.3	1.7

7. Scharf 3–4 ranks

C = ⅔′ + ½′ + ⅓′
c° = 1′ + ⅔′ + ½′
f♯° = 1⅓′ + 1′ + ⅔′
c′ = 2′ + 1⅓′ + 1′ + 1′
f♯′ = 2⅔′ + 2′ + 1⅓′ + 1⅓′

	G⅔′	C½′	G⅓′	C¼′	G⅙′	C⅛′	G1/12′
Diameter	19.5	15.3	10.8	8.2	6.3	5.7	4.2
Mouth	13.1	11.1	7.8	5.0	4.1	3.1	2.8
Cut-up	4.7	3.2	3.1	2.3	1.8	1.8	1.5

	C	c°	c'	c''	c'''
8. Krummhorn 8′					
Shallot					
Upper diameter	17.5	13.0	7.7	6.0	5.6
Lower diameter	14.2	11.0			
Length	111.0	70.0	52.0	35.0	27.0
Reed tongue thickness	.54–.65	.45	.22–.24	.20	.14
Cone diameter					
Larger	31.2	26.7	23.2	20.0	18.6
Smaller	15.3	14.0	12.5	12.3	10.5
Cone length					
Lower	208.0	150.0	97.0	70.0	59.0
Upper	100.0	59.0	49.0	31.0	15.5

PEDAL

1. Prinzipal 16′, C, D, E inside case, fir; from F in Prospekt

	F♯	c°	c'
Diameter	174.0	145.0	89.0
Mouth	137.0	113.0	67.0
Cut-up	51.0	32.0	23.0

2. Oktave 8′, Wilhelmy, 1775, utilizing older material; replaced Schnitger Bourdon 8′

	C	c°	c'
Diameter	139.0	83.0	45.0
Mouth	104.0	59.5	33.3
Cut-up	37.0	16.7	11.7

3. Oktave 4′

	C	c°	c'
Diameter	80.5	46.5	28.5
Mouth	59.5	35.0	20.2
Cut-up	17.0	12.2	6.8

4. **Nachthorn 2′, von Beckerath, reconstructed after Schnitger scalings**

5. **Rauschpfeife 2 ranks, von Beckerath, reconstructed utilizing older material**

$C = 2\frac{2}{3}' + 2'$

6. **Mixtur 4–5 ranks, von Beckerath, utilizing older material**

$C = 1\frac{1}{3}' + 1' + \frac{2}{3}' + \frac{1}{2}'$
$c^{\circ} = 2' + 1\frac{1}{3}' + 1' + \frac{2}{3}'$

7. **Posaune 16′**

	C	c°	c'
Shallot			
Upper diameter	27.6	18.2	13.2
Lower diameter	22.5	15.0	11.0
Length	182.0	112.0	82.0
Tongue thickness	.97	.64	.42
Resonator			
Diameter	180.0	140.0	95.0
Length	3645.0	1890.0	900.0

8. **Trompete 8′**

	C	c°	c'
Shallot			
Upper diameter	18.0	15.0	11.0
Lower diameter	14.5	12.0	9.0
Length	114.0	82.0	55.0
Tongue thickness	.55	.45	.25
Resonator			
Diameter	135.0	95.0	68.0
Length	1830.0	952.0	460.0

9. **Cornet 2′, actually from a Clarion 2′, reconstructed by von Beckerath utilizing older material**

Bibliography

Andersen, Poul-Gerhard. *Organ Building and Design*, translated by Joanne Curnutt. London: George Allen and Urwin, 1969; New York: Oxford University Press, 1969.

Blume, Friedrich. *Protestant Church Music*. New York: W. W. Norton, 1974.

Cremer, Ufke. "Die Orgel in der Ludgerikirche." In *400 Jahre Reformation in Norden*, edited by W. Schomerus. Norden, 1927. Pp.75–89.

de Groot, Adrianus. "Een Tekening van Arp Schnitger?" *De Mixtuur* 3 [Baarn] (July 1971): 38–41.

Edskes, Bernhardt H. "Nieuw Scheemda." In *Arp Schnitger en zijn werk in het Groningerland*, edited by H. A. Edskes, Renske Koning, and H. F. W. Kruize. Groningen: Stichting Groningen Orgelland, #1, 1975. Pp.15–43.

Edskes, Cor H. *De Nagelaten geschriften van de orgelmaker Arp Schnitger (1648–1719)*. Sneek: Boeijenga, 1968. Pp.29–71.

———. "Die Orgelbauerfamilie Huss." In *Die Huss-Orgel in Stade*, edited by Helmut Winter. Hamburg: Karl Dieter Wagner, 1979. Pp.19–25.

Edskes, Cor H. and Helmut Winter. "Technische Angaben." In *Die Schnitger-Orgel in Cappel*, edited by Helmut Winter. Hamburg: Karl Dieter Wagner, 1977. Pp.16–32.

Edskes, Cor H., Helmut Winter, and Jürgen Ahrends. "Technische Angaben." In *Die Huss-Orgel in Stade*, edited by Helmut Winter. Hamburg: Karl Dieter Wagner, 1979. Pp.33–48.

Fock, Gustav. "Arp Schnitger Beziehungen zu Neuenfelde." In *900 Jahre Neuenfelde*. Hamburg, 1959.

———. *Arp Schnitger und seine Schule*. Kassel: Bärenreiter, 1974.

Gascoigne, Bamber. *The Christians*. New York: William Morrow & Company, Inc., 1977. Pp.130–72.

Haacke, Walter. *Orgeln in aller Welt*. Boston: Crescendo Publishers, 1965.

Hill, Arthur George. *The Organ-Cases and Organs of the Middle Ages and Renaissance*. London, 1883, 1891; Buren, The Netherlands: Fritz Knuf, 1975.

Kaufmann, Walter. *Die Orgeln des alten Herzogtums Oldenburg*. Oldenburg: Gerhard Stalling Verlag, 1962.

———. *Die Orgeln Ostfrieslands*. Aurich: Verlag Ostfriesische Landeschaft, 1968.

Klimek, Lothar, ed. *Norden Ludgerikirche*. Munich and Berlin: Deutscher Kunstverlag, 1973.

Klotz, Hans. *The Organ Handbook*, translated by Gerhard Krapf. St. Louis: Concordia Publishing House, 1969.

Krüger, Liselotte. *Die Hamburgische Musikorganisation im XVII Jahrhundert*. Strassburg, 1933.

Kühn, Margarete. "History of the Building." In *Charlottenburg Palace*, translated by Henriette Beal. Berlin: Brüder Hartmann, 1937, 1976. Pp.3–25, 42–43.

Mahrenholz, Christhard. *The Calculation of Organ Pipe Scales*, translated by Andrew H. Williams. Oxford: Positif Press, 1975.

Meijer, Siewert. "Bijdragen tot de geschiedenis van het orgelmaken." *Caecelia, Algemeen muzikaal tijdschrift van Nederland* [Utrecht] 1853, 1854. Reprinted in Cor H. Edskes, *De Nagelaten geschriften van de orgelmaker Arp Schnitger (1648–1719)*. Sneek: Boeijenga, 1968. Pp.5–27.

Pape, Uwe. "Arp Schnitger." *ISO-Information* 5 [Lauffer: International Society of Organ Builders] (February 1971):357-76.

Reuter, Rudolf. *Orgeln in Westfalen*. Kassel: Bärenreiter, 1965.

Rihse, Viktor, Sonja Seggerman, and Günter Seggerman. *Klingende Schätze: Orgel-Land zwischen Elbe und Weser*. Cuxhaven: Verlag Oliva, 1958.

Schild, Fritz. *Zur Restaurierung der Orgel in Hohenkirchen*. Berlin: Pape Verlag, 1980.

Sumner, William Leslie, *The Organ: Its Evolution, Principles of Construction and Use*. London: Macdonald, 1962.

Talstra, Franz. *Langs Nederlandse Orgels (Groningen, Friesland, Drenthe*). Baarn: Bosch & Keuning NV, 1979.

Werkmeister, Andreas. *Werkmeister's Orgelprobe in English*, translated by Gerhard Krapf. Raleigh: The Sunbury, 1976.

Williams, Peter. *The European Organ, 1450–1850*. London: Batsford, 1966; Bloomington: Indiana University Press, 1978.

Winter, Helmut, ed. "Zur Geschichte der Orgel in St. Cosmae und Damiani." In *Die Huss-Orgel in Stade*. Hamburg: Karl Dieter Wagner, 1979. Pp.5–17.

———. "Zur Geschichte der Schnitger-Orgel in Cappel." In *Die Schnitger-Orgel in Cappel*. Hamburg: Karl Dieter Wagner, 1977. Pp.3–12.

Wunderlich, Heinz. *Das Kleine Orgelbuch der Hauptkirche St. Jacobi, Hamburg*. Frankfurt am Main: Brönners Druckerei Breidenstein KG, 1977.

Notes

INTRODUCTION

1. Gustav Fock, *Arp Schnitger und seine Schule* (Kassel: Bärenreiter, 1974), pp.269 and 270.

2. Ibid., pp.268 and 269.

3. Ibid., p.269.

4. Ibid.

5. Ibid.

1. PRE-SCHNITGER PATRIARCHS

1. "Die Orgel zu Rysum" (Rysum: Evangelische-reformierte Kirchengemeinde, n.d.).

2. Walter Kaufmann, *Die Orgeln Ostfrieslands* (Aurich: Verlag Ostfriesische Landeschaft, 1968), p. 213.

3. According to Alfred Führer Orgelbau restoration, 1958.

4. Gustav Fock, *Arp Schnitger und seine Schule* (Kassel: Bärenreiter, 1974), p.44.

5. Walter Kaufmann, *Die Orgeln des alten Herzogtums Oldenburg* (Oldenburg: Gerhard Stalling Verlag, 1962), p.10.

6. Ibid., p.122.

2. MEASURE OF THE MAN

1. Gustav Fock, *Arp Schnitger und seine Schule* (Kassel: Bärenreiter, 1974), p.32. The case of this organ is extant, but the instrument has gradually been replaced by the pipe work of Johann Hinrich Klapmeyer, 1726; Johann David Busch, 1781; Johann Georg Wilhelmy, 1801; Johann Hinrich Röver, 1865; Furtwängler and Hammer, 1907; and Hillebrand, 1973.

2. Ibid., pp.115 and 116; Cor H. Edskes and Helmut Winter, "Technische Angaben," in *Die Schnitger-Orgel in Cappel*, edited by Helmut Winter (Hamburg: Karl Dieter Wagner, 1977), pp.23–32.

3. Fock, p.49.

4. Ibid., p.232.

5. Jürgen Ahrend of Loga and Cor Edskes are in the process of restoring the Groningen Martinikerk organ.

6. Fock, pp.189 and 190.

7. Cor H. Edskes, *De Nagelaten geschriften van de orgelmaker Arp Schnitger (1648–1710)* (Sneek: Boeijenga, 1968), p.41.

8. Bernhardt H. Edskes, "Nieuw Scheemda," in *Arp Schnitger en zijn werk in het Groningerland*, edited by H. A. Edskes, Renske Koning, and H. F. W. Kruize (Groningen: Stichting Groningen Orgelland, #1, 1975), pp.33 and 34.

9. Ibid., pp.80 and 81.

10. The organ was demolished in 1893, except for the case, which fell on Palm Sunday, 1942, during the same air raid that destroyed the Marienkirche organ.

11. In many cases the names of these journeymen became known merely by accident, i.e., from receipts for tips on the occasion of organ deliveries. However, there is documented information regarding 49 pupils who worked as organ builders under Schnitger, an unusually large workshop for the period. Almost without exception these pupils followed closely the principles imparted by Schnitger and helped to transmit them throughout their radius of activity, which extended beyond Schnitger's to Scandinavia, the western part of the Netherlands, and the regions around Celle, Hannover, Hildesheim, and Silesia. The more important builders include Erasmus Bielfeldt (Stade); the Busch family (Itzehoe); Matthias Dropa (Lüneburg), who in 1712–14 contributed new Pedal towers for the St. Johannis Kirche in Lüneburg; Eric German (Stockholm); Johann Adam Gundermann (Wommen/Hessen), who was Schnitger's senior journeyman in Rastede/Oldenburg; Christoph Abraham Grotius (Stade), who married the daughter of Berendt Huss; Hans Hantelmann (Lübeck); Johann Balthasar Held (Lüneburg and Stettin); Michael Hinckelmann (Thorn), who also worked as Schnitger's journeyman on the Dom organ in Lübeck; Gerhard von Holy (Esens), builder of the exquisite organ (II/20) in Marienhafe; Gottfried and Hinrich Huss, presumably sons of Berendt Huss; Lambert Daniel Kastens (Itzehoe and Copenhagen); the Klapmeyer family (Glückstadt and Oldenburg); Rudolf Meyer (Hamburg), who repaired the Marienkirche organ for Buxtehude in 1705; Johann Matthias Naumann (Hildesheim); Otto Dietrich Richborn (Hamburg), who was associated with the St. Cosmae organ in Stade; Johann Michael Röder (Berlin and Silesia); the Schnitger sons—Arp, Hans, Johann Jürgen, and the well-known Franz Caspar; Johann Hinrich Ulenkampf, who worked from 1711 in Portugal under the name João Enriques Hulenkampf and built the Faro Cathedral organ in 1715–16; and Christian Vater (Hannover), who had 27 new organs to his credit, at least twelve of which are partially extant.

12. Walter Kaufmann, *Die Orgeln des alten Herzogtums Oldenburg* (Oldenburg: Gerhard Stalling Verlag, 1962), pp.69 and 70. Fock, p.131.

13. Ibid. There is no record of the specifications of the Golzwarden organ until those noted in 1803 by J. W. Krämershoff:

First Manual (45 keys)		*Upper Manual* (41 keys)	
1. Principal	8′	1. Gedackt	8′
2. Rohrflöte	8′	2. Blockflöte	4′
3. Octave	4′	3. Octave	2′
4. Gedackt	4′	4. Nassat	1⅓′
5. Octave	2′	5. Scharf	3f.
6. Quinte	1½′	*Pedal* (23 keys)	
7. Sexquialter	2f.		
8. Mixtur	3–4f.	1. Subbass	16′
9. Cimbel	3f.	2. Octave	4′
10. Trompete	8′	3. Posaune	16′
		4. Trompete	8′
		5. Trompete	4′

The only earlier records we have are comments by Christian Vater of Hannover, who undertook repair of the bellows in 1732: "Since the bellows lie on the floor alone, the wind escapes through the roof as soon as one pumps; and it can be no more unpleasant for a criminal, condemned to the galleys on his rowing bench, than for this poor musical bellows-blower" (Kaufmann, p.70).

14. Repeated repairs to the organ occurred during the nineteenth century. J. W. Krämershoff led the way in 1807, followed by the infamous Schmids—J. G. in 1829 and J. C. in 1859. The final travesty took place in 1912, when J. M. Schmid was permitted to tear down the original organ, leaving only the Prospekt. The parish council, as in many instances, was swayed by his report of 1907: "It [the organ] consists of many screaming and screeching voices, which earlier were gladly listened to, since man did not know any better, but now are considered unbearable and cannot be used by the organist. . . ." The 1965 Alfred Führer Orgelbau rebuild incorporated the Schnitger Prospekt (Fock, p.132).

15. Staatsarchiv Oldenburg. Best. 97, #892.

16. Ibid.

17. Fock, p.264.

18. Ibid., p.138; Kaufmann, p.164.

19. Fock, p.241.

20. A restoration of the Uithuizen organ under the supervision of the Rijksdienst voor de Monumentenzorg of the Netherlands is scheduled for the near future.

21. Fock, p.201.
22. Ibid., p.203.
23. Ibid., pp.203 and 204.
24. Ibid., p.204.
25. Ibid.
26. Ibid., pp.204 and 205.
27. Ibid., p.205.
28. Ibid.
29. Ibid., p.265.
30. Siwert Meijer, "Bijdragen tot de geschiedenis van het orgelmaken," *Caecilia, Algemeen muziekaal tijdschrift van Nederland* [Utrecht], vol. 10, no. 9 (May 1, 1853): 85 and 86. Reprinted by C. H. Edskes (Sneek: Boeijenga, 1968 and 1975), pp.5 and 6.

3. DEBT TO THE PAST

1. Peter Williams, *The European Organ, 1450–1850* (London: Bodsford, 1966; Bloomington: Indiana University Press, 1978), p.106.
2. Gustav Fock, *Arp Schnitger und seine Schule* (Kassel: Bärenreiter, 1974), p.21.
3. Edskes, C. H., Helmut Winter, and Jürgen Ahrends, "Technische Angaben," *Die Huss-Orgel in Stade* (Hamburg: Karl Dieter Wagner, 1979), pp.40–48.
4. Fock, p.79.
5. Ibid., p.80; Kirchenarchiv Steinkirchen, Orgelkontrakt, 1581.
6. Ibid., p.80; Kirchenarchiv Steinkirchen, Orgelakte 513, 1; Kontrakt v. 29.5, 1784.
7. Fock, p.81.
8. Ufke Cremer, "Die Orgel in der Ludgerikirche," *400 Jahre Reformation in Norden*, edited by W. Schomerus (Norden: 1927), pp.77–82.
9. Ibid., pp.88 and 89.
10. Fock, pp.151 and 152.

4. LEGACY FOR THE FUTURE

1. Staatsarchiv Oldenburg, Best. 73, #4872, Dedesdorf Kirchenrechnung, 1676.
2. Gustav Fock, *Arp Schnitger und seine Schule* (Kassel: Bärenreiter, 1974), p.133.
3. Walter Kaufmann, *Die Orgeln des alten Herzogtums Oldenburg* (Oldenburg: Gerhard Stalling Verlag), p.53.
4. Staatsarchiv Oldenburg, Best. 73, #12040, Strückhausen Orgelbaurechnung, 1698.
5. Staatsarchiv Oldenburg, Best. 73, #6772, Ganderkesee Orgelbaurechnung, 1699.

6. Fock, p.135.

7. Staatsarchiv Oldenburg, Best. 73, #6772, Ganderkesee Orgelbaurechnung, 1699.

8. Kaufmann, p.68.

9. Orgelbaumeister Fritz Schild, Alfred Führer Orgelbau.

10. Staatsarchiv Oldenburg, Best. 73, #10489, Orgelrechnung Rastede, 1709.

11. Ufke Cremer, "Urkunden zur Geschichte der Norder Schnitgerorgel," in *Heim und Herd*, supplement to *Ostfriesischen Kurier* (Norden), May 24, 1930.

Glossary of German Technical Terms

Abstrakt	tracker
Abstraktenkamm	tracker guide
Aliquot	mutation
angedrückte (Labium)	pressed-in (mouth), as opposed to soldered-in
angelötet	soldered on
Ansauggeräusch	sucking-in noise
Arm (Well-)	square, square arm, trundle arm
aufschlagend	striking (reeds)
Aufschnitt	cut-up
Auslöser	cancel piston
Balg	bellow
Balg (Pneumatik-)	motor
Barker-Hebel	Barker lever
Bart (Seiten-)	ear
Basslage	bass position
Becher	resonator
belederte Kappen	leathered caps
Blei	lead
Breite	width
Brustwerk	"breast work": division located immediately above the console in a cupboardlike enclosure with doors

Chororgel	chancel organ
Damm	bar
Diskant	treble
Diskantlage	treble position
Disposition	specification
Druckknopf	piston
Durchmesser	diameter
durchschlagend	free (reeds)
durchstecher	running
Eiche	oak
Elfenbein	ivory
eingelötet	soldered in
Empore	gallery
Endintonation	final voicing
entlastetes Spielventil	assisted pallet
Falte	fold
auswärtsgehend	outward-hinged fold
einwärtsgehend	inward-hinged fold
Feder	spring
Feld (Prospekt)	flat or field
Filz und Tuch	felt and cloth
Flachfelder	open fields or flats
flexibles Verbindungstück	flexible connecting flange
freie Kombination	free combination
freistehend	unenclosed
funktionssichere Kontakte im Spieltisch	top-working contacts in the console
Fuss	pipe-foot
Fussloch	foot hole
Gebläse	blower
gedackt	stopped
Gehäuse	case
Geigenregister	string stops
Gruntstimmen	basic tones
halbiert	halved

Halterbrett	rackboard
Hauptwerk	"head work": main division, referred to occasionally before 1700 as "manual"
Heuler	cipher
Holz	wood
Holzschnitzereien	wood carving
Horizontalbalg	horizontal bellow
Hut (Pfeifen-)	canister-stopper
Inneres der Orgel	interior of the organ
Intonation	voicing
Kanzelle	groove
Kanzellenschiede	bar
Kegel	cone-valve
Kegellade	cone-valve chest
Kehle	shallot
Keilbalg	wedge-shaped bellow
Kern	languid
Kernfase	languid bevel
Kernspalte	flue
Kernstärke	languid thickness
Kernstich	nicking
Klangcharakteristik	character of the tonality
Klaviatur	keyboard
Kondukt	air duct
konisch	conical
Konstruktion und Bau der Orgel	design and construction of the organ
Kopf (Zungen-)	block
Koppel	coupler
Kreuzprofile	cross profile
Kronwerk	"crown work": division located high in the case above the other divisions

Kröpfung	mitre
Kunststoff	plastics
Kurzoktave	short octave
Labialpfeifen	flue pipes
Labium	mouth
Lade	chest
Länge	length
Leder	leather
Leergang	backfall
Legierung	alloy
Leim und Kleber	adhesives
Leitstifte	guide pins
löten	to solder
Magazinbalg	reservoir
Manualklaviatur	manual keyboard
Material	materials
Mechanik	mechanics
mechanische Setzerkombination	mechanical combination-setter
Mensur	pipe scale
Mensurenlisten	list of scalings
Metall	metal
Millellage	middle or center position
Mixtur	mixture
Montage	installation
Normalkopplen	direct couplers
Oberlabium	upper lip
Obertaste	sharp
Oberwerk	division placed high in the case, considered the main division where no Hauptwerk is indicated
Orgelanlage	plan of the organ
Orgelaufbau	organ structure

Pedalklaviatur	pedalboard
Pfeife	pipe
Pfeifenreihe	rank
Pfeifenstock	upperboard
Pfeifentürme	pipe towers
Pflege	maintenance
Prinzipalregister	Principal stops
Prospekt	front of the organ case
Pulpete	bush or collar
Rahmenwerk	framework
Registratur	stop action
Register	stop
Registerkanzelle	stop channel
Resonanzkörper	resonance substance
Rollschweller	crescendo roller (shoe)
Rückpositiv	unenclosed division located behind the organist, normally on the gallery railing
Rundlabium	round mouth
Schallbecher	resonator
Schaltzeiten	switch times
Schiebelkoppel	shift coupler
Schleife	slider
Schleiflade	slider wind-chest
Schöpfer	feeder bellow
Schwebungen	beats
Schwellwerk	"swell work": enclosed or expressive division
Schwellkasten	swell box
Sicherheitsventil	safety valve
sonstiges Dichtungsmaterial	other scaling materials
Sperrklappe	pallet
Sperrventil	stop-valve
Spielbarkeit	quality of playing

Spieltisch	console
Spielventil	valve (pallet)
Spitzlabium	pointed mouth
Stärke	thickness
Stecher	sticker
Stiefel	boot
Stellung der Orgel	placement of the organ
stimmen	to tune
Stimmhorn	tuning cone
Stimmkrücke	tuning spring
Stimmrolle	tuning roll
Taste	key touch
Teilungen	scales
Teilwerk der Orgel	division of the organ
Tonhöhe	pitch level
Tontraktur	tone action
Tonventilmagnet	pallet magnet
Traktur	key action
Transport	transportation
Tremulant	tremulant
Turm (Prospekt-)	tower
Umfang	compass
Unterlabium	lower lip
Untertaste	natural
Ventil	valve (pallet)
Ventilkasten	valve box
Verbund-Werkstoffe	composite materials
Versand und Montage	shipping and installation
Vorintonation	preliminary voicing
waagerecht aufgehende Tonventile	horizontally opening tone stops
Wagenschoss	heartwood
Windstärke	wall thickness
Welle	roller (expression device)

Wellenbrett	rollerboard
Winddruck	wind pressure
Winderzeugung	wind supply
Windkanal	wind trunk
Windlade	wind-chest
Windwage	wind gauge
Winkel	angle
Wippe	lever
Zinn	tin
Zugelötete Pfeifen	soldered pipes (for permanent tuning)
Zunge	reed tongue
Zungenregister	reed stops

Index of Organs for Which Specifications Are Given

Berlin, Eosander-Kapelle (Schnitger) 44
Cappel, St. Petri und St. Pauli (Schnitger) 27
Dedesdorf, St. Laurentius (Schnitger);
Pedal (Köhler) 103, 106, 107
Ganderkesee, St. Cornelius und Cyprianus (Schnitger);
Pedal (Klapmeyer, Führer, Giesecke) 110–11, 114
Glückstadt, Stadtkirche (Huss) 72
Groningen, Aa-Kerk (Schnitger) 35
Groningen, Collegium Musicum (Schnitger) 31
Groningen, Martinikerk (Schnitger) 32–33
Magdeburg, St. Johannis (Schnitger) 34
Neuenfelde, St. Pankratius ((Schnitger) 81
Nieuw Scheemda, Hervormde Kerk (Schnitger) 36
Norden, St. Ludgeri (Schnitger) 93–94
Oederquart, St. Johannis (Schnitger) 26
Osteel, St. Werenfridus (Evers) 10
Pieterburen, Hervormde Kerk (Schnitger) 36
Rastede, St. Ulrich (Schnitger) 115–16
Stade, St. Cosmae (Huss and Schnitger) 77
Sengwarden, St. Georg (Kröger) 14
Steinkirchen (Hoyer and Schnitger) 83–84
Strückhausen, St. Johannes (Schnitger) 109
Uithuizen, Hervormde Kerk (Schnitger) 42

General Index

(Numbers in bold type indicate plates.)

Abbehausen, 48, 49
Accum, 40, **67**
Agricola, Rudolf, 31, 33
Ahrend, Jürgen, 76, 93
Altenbruch, 79, 89
Altenkirchen. *See* Strückhausen
Altes Land, 25, 28
Anton II, Count, 13
Anton Günther II, Count, 13, 14
Assel, 25

Barthold, M., 30
Beckerath, Rudolf von. *See* von Beckerath, Rudolf
Berlin
  Charlottenburg, 43, 45
  Dom, 45–48
  Eosander-Kapelle, 43–46, 48, **70**
  Oranienburg, 44–47
  Potsdam, 44–47
  Royal Palace-Knight's Chapel, 43–46
  St. Nikolai, 43
  St. Sebastian, 43
Berne, 12
Berner, Johann Adam, 12, 13
Bernhard, Christoph, 11, 78
Bielfeldt, Erasmus, 25, 150
Blexen, 12
Bockelmann, Christian, 13
Bockelmann, Hans the Elder, 11
Borstel, 25, 28
Bosch-Sandershauser, 110
Bremen, 31, 49
  Dom, 37, 38
  St. Ansgari, 10
  St. Martini, 13
  St. Stephani, 9, 13, 28, 37
Bülkau, 25
Busch, Johann Dietrich, 117, 150
Buxtehude, 39, 112
Buxtehude, Dietrich, 30, 41, 43

Cahman, Hans Henric, 11, 78
Cappel, 26, 27, **51**
Celle, 15
Cernitz, Ulrich, 11
Christian V, King, 39, **66**
Chrysander, Friedrich, 12
Clausthal-Zellerfeld, 39, 112
Cremer, Ufke, 85
Cropp, Hermannus, 13, 14

Damme, Johan ten. *See* ten Damme, Johan
Dargun, 39, 112
Dedesdorf, 37, 102–108, **119–121**, 132–40
de Dominis, Thidericus, 8
de Koff, J., 33
Delmenhorst, 13, 39
de Mare, Andreas, 8, 9, 31, 33, 71, 85, 93
de Mare, Marten, 8, 9
Denmark, 11
Dominis, Thidericus de. *See* de Dominis, Thidericus
Dreas, Petrus, Pastor, 106, 107
Dropa, Matthias, 150
Druckenmüller, Johann Diedrich, 91, 92

Eilsum, 40
Eitzen, Claus von. *See* von Eitzen, Claus
Elmshorn, 79
Emden, 8, 9
Emedensis, Johannes, 8
England, 4, 31
Eppendorf, 102
Esenshamm, 102
Estebrügge, 28
Evers, Edo, 8, 10, 71, 85, 89, 93

Fedderwarden, 40
Finckh, Johann Henricus von. *See* von Finckh, Johann Henricus
Flensburg, 4
Fock, Gustav, 76, 123
Freiburg, 25
Friedrich I, King, 43, **69**
Friedrich Wilhelm I, King, 45, 48
Fritzsche, Gottfried, 11, 71, 79
Fritzsche, Hans Christoph, 11, 78
Führer, Alfred, 108, 113, 114, 118, 132, 139, 151
Furtwängler and Hammer, 93, 94, 108
Furtwängler, Philipp, 79, 84

Ganderkesee, 39, 102, 110–15, **122**
German, Eric, 150
Glückstadt, 15, 71, 72, 79
Golzwarden, 25, 37, **63**, 151
Göthe, Eosander von. *See* von Göthe, Eosander
Groningen, 39, 112
  Aa-Kerk, 33, 35
  Academie-or-Broerkerk, 33
  Collegium Musicum, 31
  Lutherse Kerk, 102
  Martinikerk, 31, 32, 150
Grotius, Christoph Abraham, 150
Guericke, Otto von. *See* von Guericke, Otto
Gundermann, Johann Adam, 117, 150

Hagelberg, 31
Hamburg, 5, 10–12, 13, 42
  Pesthofkirche, 79
  St. Gertrudis, 28, 39, 42
  St. Jacobi, 11, **20**, 71
  St. Johannis-Klosterkirche, 26
  St. Katharinen, 11
  St. Michaelis, 28
  St. Nikolai, 11, 28, 30, 38, 79
  St. Pauli, 28, 79
  St. Petri, 11, 28
Hammelmann, 13
Hammerschmidt, Andreas, 11
Hantelmann, Hans, 37, 150
Held, Balthasar, 30, 150
Himmelpforten, 25
Hinckelmann, Michael, 150
Hinsch, Albert Antonius, 33, 37
Hof des Orgelbauers, 28, **99**
Hohenkirchen, 12, 29, **57**
Hollern, 28
Holstein, 28
Holy, Gerhard von. *See* von Holy, Gerhard
Hoyer, Dirk, 10, 81, 83
Hude, 12
Huss, Berendt, 14, 15, 25, 40, 71, 72, 73
Huss, Elias Otto, 15, 108
Huss, Gottfried, 15, 150
Huss, Henrich, 40, 79, 150

Jade, 39, 45
Jever, 12, 13, 29, 39, 40
Johansen, Jaspar, 10
Jork, 25, 28

Karl Wilhelm, Duke, 39
Kastens, Lambert Daniel, 43, 150
Kayser, Joachim, 29, 39, 40
Kemper, Karl, 80
Klapmeyer, Daniel, 79
Klapmeyer, Johann Henrich, 113, 114, 150
Kloster Berge, 39, 112
Koch, Gerhard, 48
Koff, J. de. *See* de Koff, J.
Köhler, Eilert, 107
Krämershoff, Johann Wilhelm, 12, 107, 108, 117, 151
Kröger, Gerd, 13, 14
Kröger, Hermann, 14, 15

Langwarden, 14, **23–24**
Leer, 102, 118
Leichel, Friedrich, 37
Lohman, H. S. G., 37
Lohman, Nicolaus Albertus, 33

Lübeck
  Dom, 30, 37, **66**, 150
  Marienkirche, 30, 31, 41, 43, **58**
  St. Aegidienkirche, 80
Lübeck, Vincent, 30, 49, 73, 74, 76, **97**
Lüdingworth, 26, 27, 79, 89
Lüneburg, 11, 13

Magdeburg
  St. Jakobi, 39
  St. Johannis, 33, 34, 37, **59**
  St. Petri, 39
  St. Ulrich, 39
Mare, Andreas de. *See* de Mare, Andreas
Marienhafe, 8
Meijer, Allert, 37
Mensingeweer, 37, **65**
Metzler and Söhne, 35, 131
Meyer, Rudolf, 42, 150
Middelstum, 102
Mill, Lampeler van. *See* van Mill, Lampeler
Millensis, Johannes, 8
Mittelnkirchen, 28, 79
Moscow, 4, 31, 37

Naumann, Johann Mattias, 39, 150
Nette, Johann, 30, 43
Neuenfelde, 2, 28, 30, 37, 49, 78–81, 90, **98**
Neuenkirchen, 28
Niehoff, Hendrik, 10
Nieuw Scheemda, 35, 36, **62**, 131–32
Noordbroek, 35, **60–61**
Norden, 9, 10, 14, 29, 30, 79, 85–94, **99**, 118

Ochsenwerder, 40
Oeckelen, Petrus van. *See* van Oeckelen, Petrus
Oederquart, **ii**, 25, 26, 149
Oldenbrok, 102
Oldenburg, 5, 8, 9, 12–15, **22**, 25, 28, 37, 115; St. Lamberti, 12–15, 39
Orgelbewegung, 93
Osteel, 10, **18–19**
Ostfriesland, 5, 8, 9, 13, 28, 40
Ott, Paul, 30, 76, 77, 80, 93
Otte, Gertrud. *See* Schnitger, Gertrud Otte
Otterndorf, 11, 29

Pellworm, 48
Pieterburen, 36, 37, **64–65**
Portugal, 4, 41
Praetorius, Jacob, 11
Praetorius, Johann, 11

Radeker (Ratje), Johan, 37
Rastede, 12, 102, 115–18
Ratje, Johan. *See* Radeker, Johan
Reformation, 5
Richborn, Joachim, 30
Richborn, Otto Dietrich, 74, 150
Rist, Johann, 11
Röder, Michael, 49, 150
Röver, Henrich, 80, 84
Röver, Johann Henrich, 75, 80, 84
Rysum, 8, **16**

Sandesneben, 102
Sauerbrey, Johann Wilhelm, 74, 75
Scharmbeck, 25
Scheemda, 8, **17**
Scheidemann, Heinrich, 11
Scherer, Hans, the Elder, 10, 11, 71, 72
Scherer, Hans, the Younger, 10, 72
Scherer, Jacob, 10
Schmalenfleth, 25
Schmid, J. C., 108, 110, 113, 118, 151
Schmid, J. G., 108, 113, 117, 151
Schmid, J. M., 110, 113, 151
Schmit, Hermannus (Hermanno), 86, 90, 91, 118
Schnitger, Agneta, 28
Schnitger, Anna Elisabeth Diekmanns Koch, 48, 49
Schnitger, Arp: signatures, 1; quotations from, 1, 2, 39, 49, 50; children, 1, 28, 29, 33, 37, 40, 49, 90, 150; correspondence, 1, 3, 4, 45, 47, 48; coat of arms, **3**; wives, 3, 28, 40, 48, 49; organ-building privileges, 4, 39–41; locations of organ projects, **6, 7,** 123–30; birthplace, 25; early period (1680–89), 25–31; residences, 25, 28, 37, 42, 43, 49, **99**; rivalry with Kayser, 29, 39, 40; dealings with Buxtehude,

Schnitger, Arp (*cont.*)
30, 31, 41; collaboration with Lübeck, 30, 49, 73, 74; middle period (1690–99), 31–40; organ construction practices, 33, 71, 79, 89–91, 102–103; contracts, 38, 85, 103–106, 108, 112, 115–17; late period (1700–19), 40–50; Court Organ Builder, Berlin, 44–47; burial place, 49
Schnitger, Arp (son), 1, 28, 40, 90, 150
Schnitger, Catharina, 29
Schnitger, Franz Caspar, 28, 33, 37, 49, 150
Schnitger, Gertrud Otte, 3, 28, 40
Schnitger, Hans, 28, 40, 90, 150
Schnitger, Johann Jürgen, 28, 150
Schortens, 29, **52–55**
Schütz, Heinrich, 11
Schwei, 37, 102
Selsingen, 79
Sengwarden, 12–14, **20**
Sieburg, Jodocus (Jost), 13, 85
Sieburg, Johann, 13
Slegal, Cornelius, 8, 9, 14
Slegal, Michael, 8, 9, 14
Sophie Charlotte, Queen, 43, **69**
Spain, 41
Stade, 15
St. Cosmae, 25, 30, 72–78, **95–97**
St. Wilhadi, 25
Steinkirchen, 11, 28, 29, 81–84, 90, **100, 101**, 140–45
Stellwagen, Friedrich, 11
Stettin, 2, 4
Stolzenberg, Henrich Bernhard, 86, 90
Strückhausen, 37, 102, 108–10
Sweden, 11
Swedish-Danish war, 40
Sweelinck, Jan Pieterszoon, 11

Tappe, Peter, 74
ten Damme, Johan, 8
Tettens, 12
The Netherlands, 5, 33, 35
Thirty Years' War, 1, 5, 11, 85
Tielcke, Joachim, 12
Twielenfleth, 28

Uithuizen, 41, 42, **68**, 112, 151
Ulenkampf, Johann Henrich, 38, 41, 150

van Mill, Lampeler, 8
van Oeckelen, Petrus, 33
Vater, Christian, 150, 151
Verbeeck, Adam, 33
Verbeeck, Antonius, 33
Vogel, Gregorius, 10
von Beckerath, Rudolf, 80, 83, 84
von Eitzen, Claus, 79, 82
von Finckh, Johann Henricus, 2, 78
von Göthe, Eosander, 43, 71
von Guericke, Otto, 33
von Holy, Gerhard, 40, 150

Westerstede, 39
Wichardt, Johann, 107, 115
Wiedeburg, J. D., 74, 76
Wilde, Antonius, 11, 28, 72
Wilhelmshaven, 108
Wilhelmshaven-Heppens, 40
Wilhelmy, Georg Wilhelm, 74, 82–84
Wilhelmy, Johann Georg, 74, 75, 84
Wittmund, 29, **56**

Zwingli, 5
Zwolle, 49